From Recreation to Re-creation
New Directions in Parks and Open Space System Planning

MEGAN LEWIS, AICP, GENERAL EDITOR

TABLE OF CONTENTS

Preface by Megan Lewis, AICP...iii

Chapter 1. Defining Parks and Park Systems by Lee Springgate...................................1
Chapter 2. Park System Functions and Services by Mary Eysenbach.........................15
Chapter 3. How Do You Effectively Assess a Community's Need for Parks
            and Open Space? by David Barth, AICP 39
Chapter 4. Parks and Open Space System Plans by Megan Lewis, AICP.....................57
Chapter 5. Creating and Maintaining Parks: Funding and Other Means
            by Peter Harnik 75
Chapter 6. Recommendations for Integrating Park and Open Space Planning
            in Overall Community Planning by Megan Lewis, AICP, and
            Mary Eysenbach 89

Appendix A. Developing a Needs Assessment: The Oviedo, Florida,
            Case Study by David Barth, AICP 95
Appendix B. Park Plans Matrices...111

CD-ROM Contents: Eleven Briefing Papers Concerning the Various Roles of Urban Parks
Volume 1.   How Cities Use Parks for Community Revitalization
Volume 2.   How Cities Use Parks for Community Engagement
Volume 3.   How Cities Use Parks for Economic Development
Volume 4.   How Cities Use Parks to Create Safer Neighborhoods
Volume 5.   How Cities Use Parks for Green Infrastructure
Volume 6.   How Cities Use Parks to Help Children Learn
Volume 7.   How Cities Use Parks to Improve Public Health
Volume 8.   How Cities Use Parks for Arts and Cultural Programs
Volume 9.   How Cities Use Parks to Promote Tourism
Volume 10. How Cities Use Parks for Smart Growth
Volume 11. How Cities Use Parks for Climate Change Management

What This PAS Report Brings to the Literature about Parks and Open Space Planning

By Megan Lewis, AICP

"All great cities in this world, where people want to live, have a great park system."
—*Dr. John Crompton, Texas A&M University*

For more than 150 years, cities in the U.S. have designed and planned urban park and open space systems. Starting with the first major city park, Central Park in New York City, and culminating most recently with Millennium Park in Chicago, grand urban parks capture the imagination, attract visitors nationally and internationally, and provide lasting experiences and memories for all who visit them.

But urban parks include more than these major places. They are the small neighborhood parks where new families take their babies to experience nature for the first time. They are the large forested areas within cities that provide multiple benefits beyond those easily classified as "recreation." They are the water's edge resources that provide environmental benefits, such as stormwater management and erosion control. They are the boulevards, trails, and other green linear connections that link together open spaces. They are, in essence, the system of green resources that help define a community and guide its growth and development.

All too often when park systems are discussed, they are considered synonymous to—and interchangeable with—recreation facilities. Various factors have created this confusion. Since the 1970s, funding sources for parks have frequently been attached to constructing certain facilities—playgrounds, ball fields, or tennis courts, for example. Parks have become "loaded" with these uses, thus creating a whole generation of users who think of parks as primarily providing recreation. Also, urban open spaces are places not "on the tax roles" for revenue purposes, so they often need to have an identifiable function to show they have value. Recreation is something considered tangible, identifiable, and perhaps most significant, quantifiable.

But perhaps the main reason recreation is emphasized is that many people believe the park system's primary function is to meet the recreation and leisure needs of community residents and visitors. This statement is seemingly benign, and perhaps even fits well within the concept of land-use planning, which seeks to provide for the needs of stakeholders, but in the case of parks, nontraditional stakeholders are plentiful and need to be considered. How do you involve wildlife in a planning process? Where does the consideration of the needs of the watershed fit into the model? How can the future elderly population express their need to view trees and thus live a longer, happier life?

To create truly successful park systems, park planning needs to incorporate the needs of these stakeholders into the process—in essence, bring together the broad, inclusive approach of comprehensive planning and the natural system mindset of environmental planning in a new approach to park system planning. This new approach can be viewed as a move away from primarily "recreation" to the idea of "re-creation," or creating places that allows individuals to "re-create" themselves and their relationship to nature. This report elaborates on several trends the field of parks and open space planning, and the authors hope to successfully shift the discussion about such planning to include the importance of re-creation.

PARK PLANNING GUIDANCE

When I began to conceive this report, I reviewed literature considered to be the primary resources for planning for parks and open space, to see what guidance these materials had for taking park system planning into a new direction.

Four main resources are often cited as "the" park planning publications:

1. *Recreation Planning and Design* (Gold 1980)

2. *Planning Parks for People* (Hultsman, Cottrell, and Zales-Hultsman 1987)

3. *Park Planning Guidelines* (Fogg 1990) (a new edition, renamed *Park, Recreation & Leisure Facilities Site Planning Guidelines*, by the same author, was published in 2005)

4. *Park, Recreation, Open Space and Greenway Guidelines* (Mertes and Hall 1996).

This list is not meant to be exhaustive, but rather to highlight the most often cited sources on park planning information. Other documents and reports on this topic exist, but they are not in wide circulation. I welcome any comments on additional literature that should be considered part of the principal body of information about park planning.

Recreation Planning and Design

Gold focuses on the process and products of urban recreation planning. He discusses recreation planning in the planning tradition, including the importance of a parks, recreation, and open space element in a community's comprehensive plan. He supports a planning period of 20 years, mirroring the comprehensive plan and capital improvement plan cycles.

Certain parts of this publication are understandably dated, however. For example, public participation, which is an integral part of any planning process, is presented as a new idea in this book. Also, the focus is quite heavy on the provision of recreation; Gold describes parks and recreation planning as the "systematic way of anticipating, causing, preventing, or monitoring change related to the provision of public and private leisure opportunities" (p. 22). And he says that a park and recreation plan is "an expression of a community's objectives, needs, and priorities for leisure space, service, and facilities" (p. 59). While he does note that parks and recreation are only one possible use of open space, he emphasizes that open space should not be a substitute for recreation provision. When looking for a publication that discusses park planning in the language of urban planning, this publication certainly meets that need, but the author views and discusses this process as one parallel to and not integrated with a comprehensive planning process.

Planning Parks for People

The title of this publication might lead the reader to believe that the authors are going to provide a broad perspective about parks and the place of parks in the community. The authors strongly emphasize recreation, however, and "planning," as used within the book, means site planning. The authors define parks broadly but say, "(T)his book is concerned primarily with resource-based, outdoor recreation areas" (p. 6). The authors' focus is on site-specific issues; the book does not provide broad planning guidance for park system planning.

Park Planning Guidelines

The 1990 edition of this book is "intended to provide information on the physical aspects of planning large-scale, resource-oriented parks" (p. ix). The author focuses on identifying visitor demand, based on service area and park use. He also emphasizes design, particularly program design. The author presents some information on general site design, discussing such items as screening and noise barriers, and he does mention accessibility and environmentally sensitive design. While this publication provides specific guidance on certain issues and uses, like the other works listed here, it does not treat parks and open space system planning broadly. The new edition has a section on site design and managing the construction process, and it is updated to address issues that have appeared since the last publication, including the Americans with Disabilities Act, off-road vehicles, and tourism. The graphics have also been updated. The author's approach to the topic, however, is still quite similar to the one he took in the previous edition.

Park, Recreation, Open Space, and Greenway Guidelines

This publication (referred to as the NRPA guide in this PAS Report) is perhaps the most often-cited book for park planning guidance, especially when trying to determine the provision of parks. While previous editions presented standards for park creation and planning that had been taken as "gospel," the current edition has a change in philosophy. The authors provide guidance to communities so that each community can create its own custom standards rather than applying an absolute national standard. The authors also encourage communities to be more strategic in planning for parks.

The authors definitely take a broad approach to defining parks. They present the idea that "the entire community is a park and that all land uses should result in environmentally harmonious park, recreation, and open space land units" (p. 7). And they note that communities may be more interested in open space preservation and nature-based recreation than the traditional menu of activities. The trends section is particularly prescient, covering environmental, social, economic, demographic, technological, and urban pattern trends. Among the predicted implications of those trends are the following, which in part served as a catalyst for the creation of this PAS Report:

- Broader definitions of open space and green space
- Emphasis on the various "services" provided by parks and open spaces (e.g., stormwater management, transportation, revitalization, and sustainability)
- Greater focus on a benefits-driven needs assessment and the creation and identification of opportunities for joint use of facilities to reduce redundancy in service delivery
- More emphasis on comprehensive open space planning and preservation and the inclusion of parks and open space planning throughout the community's planning and development process

- Encouragement of community volunteerism and partnerships with other public, private, and nonprofit sectors for park provision and maintenance
- Acknowledgment that planning is a decision-making process, not just a physical plan

But there are shortcomings as well. While the authors discuss a system planning model, they actually develop a model for applying a systems approach to the planning of parks, recreation, open space, and pathways, and the systems approach they describe ultimately remains focused on providing recreation services to users. The authors' multiple-step planning process also seems confusing at times and to have its directives out of order. In short, the NRPA guide takes a major leap forward to define a method of planning for parks, but its strength is as a guide for identifying local needs for certain uses and conducting an inventory of resources.

HOW IS THIS PAS REPORT DIFFERENT?

My review of these four publications led to two conclusions:

1. A wealth of information exists about designing specific parks and recreation facilities, and within this body of literature, "planning" most often refers to site planning.

2. The main body of literature that does speak specifically to park system planning usually has a recreation bias and an emphasis on identifying user needs.

In short, specific guidance on planning for parks and open space systems in a manner similar to planning for other community resources is simply not available.

Planners know planning. Park professionals know parks. Given this realization, APA opted to make this third report in the City Parks Forum PAS Report series a report in which the two disciplines got together and brought the collective professional strengths of each to a manual about how to create a comprehensive, communitywide park and open space system planning process.

Toward that end, the project enlisted the expertise of several park professionals from across the country, from the public, private, and nonprofit sectors, to serve as coauthors of this PAS Report. I asked each person to write based on their experiences and research, with the emphasis on moving park system planning in a new direction.

In defining what might be considered the dominant park movement today, Lee Springgate proposes in the report's first chapter that parks should be viewed as one component of a park system, with recreation facilities, natural resource sites, cultural and historic sites, forests and farms, and streetscapes as examples of additional park system components. This approach, while similar to comprehensive planning, in which a community's planners address its many components, is still novel for parks inasmuch as it deemphasizes recreation as the primary outcome and broadens the idea of "parks" to be many things. Springgate also discusses criteria that could be used to determine if parks—and thus the park system—are successful.

Among the things that parks can be are the various functions and services that parks perform for our communities. As Mary Eysenbach notes in Chapter 2, parks are "places and spaces" that can meet broader community needs and goals if they are reconsidered in that light. She covers numerous park functions, including economic development, public health, green infrastructure, cultural expression, urban form, civic and social capital, education, and, of course, recreation. She stresses that each community must involve residents to determine how parks are actually used in order to determine each park's set of functions.

When planning for parks and open spaces, all communities must first identify the "gaps" in their current system. To do this, the most common approach is to conduct a needs assessment. In Chapter 3, David Barth presents a method of doing this—called triangulation—that serves to differentiate between community needs and community priorities. Specifically, triangulation calls for a method that incorporates data using an approach that applies three techniques—anecdotal, quantitative, and qualitative. Each provides a different way of obtaining stakeholder input and the information necessary to do an accurate needs assessment.

For a needs assessment to have results, it should be part of an overall planning process. In Chapter 4, I discuss the current state of comprehensive parks and open space planning in the U.S. In conducting my initial research, I found that not all the cities known for their park systems have a parks and open space plan. Among those that do have a plan, however, the plans do indeed seem to address several of the trends noted above. Communities are beginning to see parks more broadly and to plan for them as a "green system" that is as valuable as the other land uses that comprise them. Innovative approaches to stakeholder involvement and financing are also emerging.

In Chapter 5, Peter Harnik notes that, while various financing mechanisms exist for the creation of parks (e.g., donation, purchase (either by the parks department or another agency), or revenue capture from existing or new revenue streams), finding adequate resources for park maintenance is often a major challenge. Harnik echoes the NRPA publication in the importance of cultivating volunteers and others outside the parks department to support the maintenance of parks.

From defining parks to describing their many benefits and services to examining how they might best be included in community planning and capital financing, this report deals with the key issues in park planning today. In Chapter 6 Mary Eysenbach and I summarize the conclusions from each author and attempt to integrate them into the community planning process, which we define as including visioning and goal setting, plan making, management tools, public investment, other implementation measures, and policy change. We draw on our experiences as a park professional and planner, respectively, to put forth our suggestions.

Finally, information that complements the authors' findings in this PAS Report is included in two appendices and on a CD-ROM insert. For those not familiar with the needs assessment process, David Barth, author of Chapter 3, has developed a case study showing the process used in Oviedo, Florida, and included as Appendix A. Appendix B provides a matrix of the park plans that I researched for my discussion in Chapter 4, providing more detail about the 26 factors I reviewed in each plan. On the CD-ROM are the briefing papers prepared as part of APA's City Parks Forum. This research project involved working with mayors from 25 cities to identify park issues in their communities and to develop guidance for their communities to help them address their particular situation. These briefing papers (the series is called "How Cities Use Parks") cover numerous issues, including community revitalization, economic development, crime, public health, and smart growth. A special issue, on the connection between parks and climate change management, was produced at the end of 2006. These papers have proven useful to many when they are working with community decision makers. They help further the case that parks are necessary, integral elements of successful places.

A FINAL WORD

Readers may notice that the authors of the chapters in this PAS Report do not always agree with each other. When using this report, you should consider it to be an anthology of ideas from which you may draw information for your own needs in order to make your own conclusions and to develop your own method of parks and open space system planning. A major point of agreement among the authors is the need to customize a park system to meet a particular community's needs. The same goes for the information included in this PAS Report—the authors do not tell you exactly how to define a park nor do they describe the specific method you must use to plan for a park system in your community. You will not find a formula here—in fact, formulas are what got park planning into trouble in the past.

I am fortunate in that my office overlooks Grant Park and Lake Michigan. As I have worked on this report I have seen the lakefront change from an emerging spring landscape, to a festive place for the thousands of people enjoying numerous special events, such as the Taste of Chicago (held annually around the 4th of July), to a vibrant exhibit of fall colors. I think about how Daniel Burnham, in his 1909 *Plan of Chicago*, designated the Lake Michigan waterfront to be available for the "enjoyment" of all people. When Burnham used the word "enjoy," I wonder if he could imagine how broadly that might be interpreted in the future. By creating a system of parks and boulevards, and making a plan that considered these resources as part of an interconnected system, he did indeed create a green network that Chicagoans enjoy in a multitude of ways. I hope that this report allows you to apply that word, enjoy, in a way that anticipates the numerous benefits that parks and open space provide for people today and for generations to come.

REFERENCES FOR PREFACE

Burnham, Daniel. 1909. *Plan of Chicago*. Chicago: Commerce Club.

Fogg, George. 1990. *Park Planning Guidelines*. Arlington, Va.: National Recreation and Park Association.

————. 2005. *Park, Recreation and Leisure Facilities Site Planning Guidelines*. Arlington, Va.: National Recreation and Park Association.

Gold, Seymour M. 1980. *Recreation Planning and Design*. New York: McGraw-Hill.

Hultsman, John, Richard L. Cottrell, and Wendy Zales-Hultsman. 1987. *Planning Parks for People*. State College, Pa.: Venture Publishing.

Mertes, James D. and James R. Hall. 1996. *Park, Recreation, Open Space and Greenway Guidelines*. Arlington, Va.: National Recreation and Park Association.

CHAPTER 1

Defining Parks and Park Systems

By Lee Springgate

What is a park, and why is that an important question? The answer, while deceptively complex, is of vital importance to park users, managers, and decision makers. The *Oxford English Dictionary* online version defines a park as "a large public garden in a town, used for recreation." *The Merriam-Webster Collegiate Dictionary* (2002) travels back in time to Western European influences and offers the following primary descriptions: "**1a**: an enclosed piece of ground stocked with game and held by royal prescription or grant **b**: a tract of land that often includes lawns, woodland, and pasture attached to a country house and is used as a game preserve and for recreation **2a**: a piece of ground in or near a city or town kept for ornament and recreation **b**: an area maintained in its natural state as a public property."

As a practical matter, there is no standard, widely accepted definition of a park to guide critical decisions regarding the location, development, and management of urban parks. As demonstrated by the inclusive Merriam-Webster definition, parks have evolved over time to reflect fundamental changes in society. Certainly the word "park" has been used to describe a wide array of public spaces, from athletic complexes and nature preserves to gardens and trail corridors. The term has even been adopted by the private sector and applied to an astonishing variety of spaces, including theme parks, retirement parks, recreational vehicle parks, industrial parks, and office parks.

HISTORIC INFLUENCES

Today's urban parks can trace their lineage to at least four major influences. Marina Schinz (2002), in *Visions of Paradise*, describes the first influence—the many types of formal and informal garden "schools" that evolved over the past several hundred years, including cottage, herb, rose, and kitchen gardens, as well as perennial borders and the Italian, French, and English gardens. While a detailed description of these garden types is beyond the scope of this chapter, it is important to note that they represent of range of formal and informal styles and were, for all practical purposes, the earliest urban parks. The idea of a park as a place of respite, retreat, and beauty clearly originated with these early garden types.

Ken Sherman

Urban parks can trace their lineage, in part, to the "garden" movement of the past few centuries. This movement clearly saw the park as a place of respite, retreat, and beauty. This is the Westside Community Garden in New York City.

The second influence on the development of urban parks in America is the Landscape Design School of nineteenth-century Europe. Inspired by landscape painters, designers used the organizing elements of open lawns, pathways, water bodies, groves of trees, and major earth forms to create these spaces. As opposed to the rigidly controlled and manipulated urban garden, these parks have a more relaxed style that creates scenic landscapes and allows more informal and flexible use of the land. This idealized rural landscape defined many aristocratic European estates, some of which were preserved as major public park sites.

The Landscape Design School heavily affected the work of Frederick Law Olmsted, the U.S.'s first landscape architect and park planner. Starting in the 1850s, Olmsted created parks that were spacious, informal, unstructured, and beautiful, similar in style and substance to parks he visited in Europe. These "pleasure grounds" had a clear social agenda. They were intended to elevate, inspire, and civilize. They were also passionately promoted and

The Landscape Design School was a second influence on the planning of urban parks. These parks create scenic landscapes, as this photo of Austin Town Park shows.

Eric Swanson

defended. These early American parks accommodated a variety of both structured and unstructured recreation uses, including pathways, skating rinks, and playgrounds. However, most of the space within these parks was open and accessible to all park users to engage in whatever activities they selected. The spaciousness, flexibility, and beauty that characterized these early Olmsted parks became the standard by which major urban parks were developed throughout the U.S. in the late nineteenth and early twentieth centuries.

Galen Cranz (1998), in the classic *Politics of Park Design*, documents the third major influence in the evolution of urban parks, the Reform and Recreation Facilities Eras. From 1900 to 1930, the Reform movement focused on helping inner-city residents "productively" use their leisure time. This movement focused on aggressively combating a host of social ills through the provision of enlightened programming and recreation facilities. A genuine reform zeal permeated this time, with such byproducts as the playground movement, neighborhood parks, recreation centers, and leisure programming.

Unknown

The Reform Movement of the early twentieth century suggested that parks could play a role in having inner-city residents use their time more "productively." Playgrounds, like this one in Newark, New Jersey, are an outgrowth of this philosophy.

From 1930 to 1965, the Recreation Facility Era dominated the park scene. During this period, social reform was discarded in favor of "pragmatic" considerations. The intense passion that characterized both the Landscape Design and Reform periods vanished. Planning standards arose for a wide range of facilities and programs, from sports fields and community centers to playgrounds and tennis courts. Parks became defined predominantly as repositories for recreation programs and facilities. A "good" park was one that accommodated as many recreation facilities and organized recreation uses as possible, with landscaping, aesthetics, and open space relegated to a secondary role. These recreation-oriented parks have proliferated in recent decades, particularly in suburban communities, largely because, over the past 20 to 30 years, recreation demand has skyrocketed. Everything from soccer, slow-pitch softball, and skateboarding, to bicycle trails and cultural arts has staked a claim on public parkland. This genre of park is characterized by limited and controlled public access. The majority of space is reserved for specific uses and often intensively scheduled.

Tom Evers

From about 1930 to 1965, the Recreation Facility Era meant that parks became places for recreational facilities, relegating landscaping, aesthetics, and open space to a secondary role. Among the legacies of this movement are skateboarding facilities, like this one in a Chicago park.

The final influence on the nature of the urban park is natural resources protection, driven by the unique natural resource base associated with any given jurisdiction. This desire to preserve, protect, and provide access to urban trees and forests, fresh and saltwater shorelines, viewpoints, wetlands, wildlife habitat, and other critical resources has been of paramount importance for more than 100 years. This influence certainly drives the creation and protection of state and national parks, and it received added impetus in the early 1970s with the emergence of the environmental movement. This strong need to interpret and interact with natural systems has significantly affected the development of park systems at all levels within the U.S.

A WORKING DEFINITION OF PARKS

So what differentiates a park from other private and public land holdings? What are the different type of urban parks, what is the optimum mix, and how do they relate to the broader park and open space system? Given

Another influence on all types of park development has been the desire to protect and preserve natural resources. A young man sits in the Mountains to Sound Greenway Park in Issaquah, Washington.

Dan Lamont

the expansive historical influences underpinning modern park systems, it is not easy to develop a narrow park definition. Rather than creating a concise definition, I propose using four criteria to help identify a place as a park. A park (1) is publicly accessible; (2) has identifiable boundaries; (3) contributes to overall community aesthetics; and (4) provides a community gathering place.

Publicly Accessible

Parks must be publicly accessible, regardless of ownership. Such accessibility is a great virtue and a defining characteristic of parks. Everyone is welcome whenever a park is open. Use of a park is not reserved only for specific users or eliminated because of site constraints. Parks are public goods that provide substantial public access and benefits to all.

Identifiable Boundaries

Parks are distinct geographic entities whether they stand alone or, ideally, connect with larger greenway, trail or environmental systems. They are identifiable public spaces that accommodate a wide variety of public uses. Parks are places where one can picnic with the family, play a game of soccer, fly a kite, watch people, read a book, walk, bike, fish, sail, listen to a concert—the list goes on. Regardless of the type of park one visits, a sense of freedom and spontaneity should be associated with the experience. While some park sites feature extensive recreation and cultural facilities, park managers need to be careful not to reach a tipping point in which too much space is converted to restricted uses, and the park loses its value as a public park site.

Aesthetic Places

Parks develop or preserve natural beauty. These sites can be formal, traditional spaces that provide grass, trees, flowers, public art, and similar attributes. Or they can be environmentally sensitive places characterized by protected streams, meadow grasses, wildflowers, informal pathways, and viewpoints.

Community Gathering Places

Parks host major concerts, festivals, and events. Fourth of July celebrations, arts and crafts fairs, holiday light festivals, and similar activities bring a community together, and these events often take place in public parks. In keeping with their flexible nature, parks can absorb these functions, while still maintaining their core mission of providing recreation opportunities and aesthetic space. (For further discussion on the functions and services of parks, see Chapter 2 of this PAS Report.)

PARK TYPES

Parks come in all shapes and sizes. The National Recreation and Park Association (NRPA) has developed a classification system for parks and open space as a component of its 1996 *Park, Recreation, Open Space and Greenway Guidelines.* (See Figure 1-1 on the following page.)

The following definitions are found on pages 94 and 95 of the guidelines, in the Parks, Open Space, and Pathways Classification Table. A *mini park* is "used to address limited, isolated or unique recreational needs." A *neighborhood park*, five to 10 acres in size, serves "as the recreational and social focus of the neighborhood and generally serves a radius of a quarter to half mile." A *community park*, 30 to 50 acres in size, serves two or more neighborhoods and a one-half- to three-mile radius. Its purpose is to "meet

Dennis Sheridan

A working definition of a park would include "being a place of natural beauty." This Blue Morro butterfly might be one of the "beauties" that people find in a park.

FIGURE 1-1. PARK TYPES

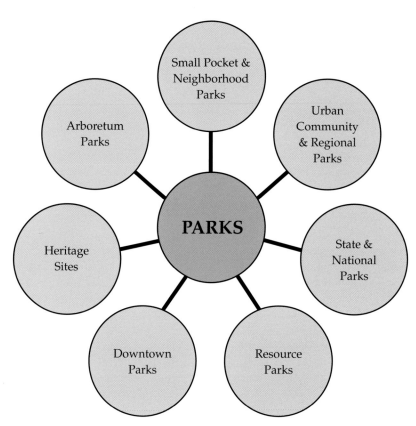

Source: The Point Wilson Group © 2006

community-based recreation needs, as well as preserving unique landscapes and open spaces." A large urban park, which is more than 50 acres and serves the entire community, is "focused on meeting community-based recreational needs, as well as preserving unique landscapes and open spaces." Missing from NRPA's classification system is a *regional park*, which typically is more than 100 acres in size, serves two or more jurisdictions, and is often managed by a county jurisdiction.

Community, large urban, and regional parks are traditional parks accommodating the widest variety of uses in the most pristine settings. They are able to provide the classic park functions while simultaneously meeting other system needs, such as regional trailheads, sports complexes, and environmental protection. These parks typically protect or create unique landscapes.

State and national parks serve a similar purpose as a regional, community, or large urban park, but on a much larger scale. These park sites are much more oriented toward preserving treasured state and national jewels, such as the Grand Canyon and Yellowstone. While state and national parks have a primary focus on resource protection and visitor experience, regional, community, and large urban parks are typically oriented toward meeting the needs of urban populations. Some notable exceptions to this are Boston and Washington, D.C., both of which have national parks within the city boundaries, which therefore function as urban parks as well as national parks.

The NRPA classification system also includes the categories of school-park and sports complex. A school-park, "depending on circumstances, combines parks with school sites to fulfill space requirements for other classes

T.W. Offut

State and national parks focus on resource protection and visitor experience. This is Cuyahoga State Park in Ohio.

of parks." A sports complex "consolidates heavily programmed athletic fields and associated facilities to larger and fewer sites strategically located throughout the community."

These two categories are interesting for two reasons. First, they acknowledge that sites heavily loaded with formal, scheduled recreation facilities should be viewed differently than a park. The school-park category is particularly important because of the potential that school sites have to meet burgeoning recreation demand. School districts have a large inventory, are geographically dispersed, have existing infrastructure, are already used for this purpose, and have the space to accommodate more recreation facilities. They also usually need improved maintenance and scheduling, which a park system can provide. Secondly, the names imply that sites intended to exclusively meet the needs of organized, scheduled recreation should be described accordingly and viewed differently with respect to other components of a larger park, recreation, and open space system.

Three additional park categories are offered for consideration. *Downtown parks* are becoming increasingly important as cities try to attract both new businesses and residents to their downtown core. These sites provide a different function than either community or large urban parks. In addition to providing a needed oasis amidst the concrete and asphalt, downtown parks are intended to provide genuine economic stimulus. This public investment often precedes a renaissance in corresponding private investment.

Resource parks incorporate unique and special physical resources, such as lakes, rivers, and ocean shorelines. These natural resources provide myriad opportunities for recreation, including boating, fishing, swimming, hiking, mountain biking, and bird watching. To enjoy and participate in these activities, one goes to these specific sites. While resource parks can be large urban or regional parks, they can also be much smaller areas that provide access to unique resources. Note that this park classification differs in substance from NRPA's natural resource area category. Its definition states that lands in this category "are set aside for preservation of significant natural resources, remnant landscapes, open space and visual aesthetics/buffering," which does not include the user aspects of such areas.

Heritage sites are areas unique and special to individual communities. They can be anything from historic dairy farms and treasured tree groves

T.W. Offut

"School-park" and "sports complex" are two park categories meant for parks that exclusively meet recreation demand, such as this school-park soccer field in Lowell, Massachusetts.

Rich Reid

Downtown parks provide both economic stimulus and relief from the "hardness" of the city center. This is Cornfield Park in East Los Angeles.

Unknown

Pritchard Park on Bainbridge Island in Washington is a resource park, meaning it incorporates unique or special resources.

to old homesteads. These places evoke a strong emotional response and provide a direct link to the past. Particularly during times of extraordinarily rapid change, it becomes even more important to protect what remains of our heritage.

Every community has an obligation to establish its own park typology that reflects its unique history and situation. Communities should view their park inventory in a comprehensive, disciplined, and systematic manner. Focus particular attention on ensuring a balance among the different type of parks available within the system. Virtually all of these park types, with their respective historical influences, have merit and value. In recent decades, however, communities have shown a propensity to provide parks "loaded" primarily with recreation facilities or encumbered by physical constraints. The Olmsted-style parks, in which the majority of space is perceived as flexible, are perhaps not fully appreciated or understood. The desire to inundate these landscapes with a wide assortment of recreation facilities seems to be growing. When these changes are allowed, the spontaneous, restorative, and aesthetic characteristics of traditional parks are discounted, and the entire park system is diminished accordingly.

PARK, RECREATION, AND OPEN SPACE SYSTEMS

Now that I have presented some criteria and methods to define parks, it is important to next place them within the larger context of an integrated park, recreation, and open space system. In addition to his early work on individual parks, Olmsted pioneered the concept of a park "system" in which boulevards and trails connect significant parklands. Olmsted referred to these systems as "pearls on a string," a concept brought to life by Boston's "Emerald Necklace" and Minneapolis's "Chain of Lakes."

Around the turn of the twentieth century, elected and appointed officials who had both the vision and courage to act aggressively on behalf of present and future generations faithfully implemented many of these systems. These leaders left a magnificent physical legacy that should inspire the current community leadership in this country. These early pioneers also provided a lesson of equal magnitude: parks need to be supported by a strong, well-articulated vision and philosophy. These leaders were passionate, committed, politically astute trailblazers.

Parks can help us maintain our connection with our past. Specifically, heritage parks recall a community's history in a special place. In Littleton, Colorado, such a place is Chambers Farm.

Nevada Weir

The idea of linkages is crucial in both a historical and contemporary sense. By connecting disparate sites via boulevards, trails, and other linear open spaces, parklands become more usable, accessible, and visible. Park systems were integrated into the overall community fabric. They connected neighborhoods, commercial areas, parks, schools, and other points of interest.

As the influences I described above became more prevalent, however, parks evolved from being the dominant element of a park system into one component of a complex parks, open space, and recreation system. New open spaces, environmental initiatives, and greenway systems were superimposed over these early park systems, and as a result urban open space systems today are asked to do more than simply provide formal and informal recreation opportunities. They are expected to shape communities and contribute to environmental quality. Wetlands, forests, wildlife corridors, farmlands, and historic sites are all among the additional resources considered to be part of an open space inventory a community should protect in a sensitive and holistic manner. These systems are expected to contribute toward water quality, flood control, clean air, wildlife preservation, and agricultural protection. Furthermore, as a system, they need to achieve multiple social benefits, including a wide array of formal recreation opportunities, while simultaneously providing connectivity, aesthetics, resource protection, neighborhood

Greenways, like Miccosukee Greenway in Tallahassee, Florida, have become part of complex park systems, helping achieve both social and natural park goals.

Anne Nelson

enhancement, and, increasingly, economic development. (See Chapter 2 for a more extensive discussion of these and other functions.) Ideally, jurisdictions should strive for a balanced system that efficiently achieves a full range of park, recreation, and open space objectives.

FIGURE 1-2. PARK SYSTEMS

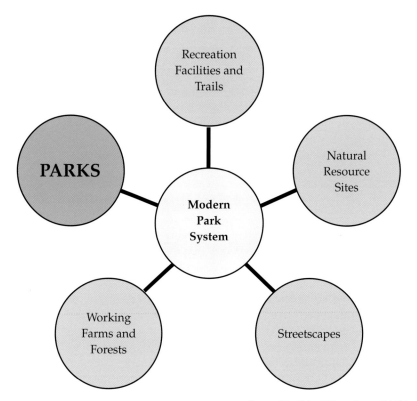

Source: The Point Wilson Group © 2006

COMPONENTS OF PARK SYSTEMS

As mentioned, parks today are one component of a broader park, recreation, and open space system. These systems may include several features; I include here what I consider to be the six major features of a park, recreation, and open space system: regional trails, critical resource sites, streetscapes, open spaces, recreation complexes, and parks.

Trails

Regional, multipurpose trails are often referred to as "linear" parks. These trails are recreation facilities that also serve as primary connectors among neighborhoods, business areas, parks, schools, and other community assets. They have become vital pieces of the greenway phenomena and serve a transportation purpose within park, open space, and recreation systems.

Resource Sites

Critical resource sites are those areas in which the majority of space is considered "natural" or environmentally sensitive. These sites may include urban forests, wildlife habitat, wetlands, steep slopes, estuaries, riparian corridors, and tidelands. The key to whether these sites are environmental parks or critical resource sites is the extent of public access and education. Areas essentially off limits to the public due to their sensitive environmental function are critical resource areas; environmental park sites are still accessible to the public.

Streetscapes

Streetscapes are becoming a critical part of most urban park and open space systems. Street trees, medians, entryways, public plazas, sidewalks, and promenades add beauty, function, and excitement to any community. For many citizens, streetscapes are their most important visual connection to the park and open space system. Streetscapes speak volumes about the community to citizens, employees, and visitors.

Open Spaces

Included within virtually all jurisdictions are a variety of valued open spaces that do not fit within the other park, natural resource, and recreation definitions. This category includes the rather eclectic mix of agricultural land, working forests, viewpoints, community gardens, arboretums, academic campuses, highway clover leafs, and institutional or corporate grounds. These areas provide aesthetic and psychological relief from urban development.

Recreation Complexes

Major recreation complexes are those sites in which nearly all of the available space is devoted to specific recreation uses available to specific users at specific times. As mentioned previously, these are either stand-alone sites devoted to a particular recreation function, such as soccer, baseball, or skateboarding, or they are school sites that meet a variety of recreation needs. In either case, the limited focus on these areas make them serve another purpose within the larger context of the park, recreation, and open space system than a park, as described in this chapter.

CRITERIA FOR SUCCESS

Parks are historically relevant, distinct spaces within the overall park, recreation, and open space system, important to the community in a number of ways. So then what constitutes a *successful* park? I have identified six criteria for park success (the order of which may vary depending upon community goals and concerns):

1. Safe and Secure
2. Well Maintained
3. Well Designed and Constructed
4. Appropriately Located
5. Socially Relevant
6. Physically Accessible

Jason Lindsay

Recreation complexes, like this baseball park in the West Lawn neighborhood in Chicago, help round out service delivery in a larger park, recreation, and open space system.

Safe and Secure

People, particularly women and children, need to feel comfortable visiting any park site. Without this fundamental condition, parks lose their support, appeal, and relevance. They simply cannot fall victim to crime, graffiti, or vandalism. Every effort needs to be made to combat these elements, from ensuring that these sites have unobstructed views from a variety of vantage points to programming the sites with an assortment of activities. Regular police and park ranger visits and interactions with park users are also important to preserve safety.

Well Maintained

Parks need to meet rigorous maintenance standards and declare by their appearance that they are valued spaces. Graffiti and vandalism must be addressed immediately, park structures and furniture of all kinds need to be repaired or replaced on a regular basis, and plant material needs to be appropriately maintained. Parks should be aesthetic spaces, elevating the appearance of the community in which they are located.

Well Designed and Constructed

Parks need to respond to the needs of a community and simultaneously protect the community's unique physical attributes. They need to be special, memorable spaces that stand the test of time. They cannot succumb to special interest demands and retain their status as a public park. Construction shortcuts should not be tolerated, because the long-term results will become obviously apparent.

Appropriately Located

Two underlying conditions need to exist for parks to add significant value to any urban community: population density and land scarcity. As populations increase in urban areas and open areas become less common, parks become extremely important to everyone's quality of life. Parks need to be located where they can meet the needs of higher-density living and provide relief from it.

Socially Relevant

Parks need to respond to and meet the needs of the community in which they are located. Cultural sensitivity needs to be reflected in these spaces so that they are, indeed, important to the people who live within their service area. They cannot be viewed as relics of another time and place and still serve their intended purpose.

Physically Accessible

Major freeways, arterials, commercial districts, water bodies, or other similar constraints should not cut off parks from intended users. Also, particular attention needs to be given to the type of land acquired for park purposes. It is not simply getting to the parks; one must be able to use the space to engage in a preferred form of activity. This differentiates a park from environmental land, greenbelts, or other open spaces. Too often, park sites are acquired only to find they are overly constrained by natural features to serve their intended purpose.

MAJOR CHALLENGES

A number of significant challenges must be met for parks to maintain their relevance in the twenty-first century. Most important is to communicate to the public and decision makers what parks are and why they are important. Park "ambassadors" need to step forward and champion the cause. A number of formal and grassroots organizations have stepped up over the past 20 years or more to do just this, from Olmsted societies to "Friends" organizations and park foundations. These organizations need to be recognized, appreciated, and involved in park system planning at both the site and system levels, and from the beginning of the process through to implementation.

Another challenge to park survival is the influence special interest groups have had on the park system planning process, at both the macro and micro levels. They are often able to dominate the political process through a variety of techniques, such as sponsoring and financing political candidates, packing public hearings, creating targeted web sites, and operating letter-writing campaigns. Without a more commonly understood and accepted definition of a park and the system in which in operates, these groups are often able to easily influence planning outcomes. Planners need to provide a counterweight with objective planning tools, such as statistically valid surveys and

Parks need to respond to the needs of a community and simultaneously protect the community's unique physical attributes. They need to be special, memorable spaces that stand the test of time.

focus groups, to reveal with much more accuracy what constituents and voters value within their community. Invariably, when communities use these methods to help decide the composition, timing, and magnitude of levies and bond measures, they experience a high degree of success.

Third, park advocates should view the need to meet other needs within the park, recreation, and open space system as an opportunity. For example, one viable strategy for meeting the organized recreation needs of a community is to fully use school district properties. Park advocates must also support initiatives that preserve critical resource lands, heritage sites, and other pieces of the open space system. In other words, to ensure that parks are provided and protected, become a champion of a full-service park, recreation, and open space system. This new focus will help increase the size of the financial pie allocated to these systems.

Fourth, park supporters need to integrate park acquisition and development proposals with other community priorities. For example, a creative mix that includes a central downtown park, plazas, rooftop parks, promenades, entryways, trails, and street trees is vital to the revitalization and vitality of central business districts. Public infrastructure investment is often the catalyst for major private sector involvement and for pursuing other community objectives, such as neighborhood enhancement and preservation of cultural and historic sites. To remain viable, parks must be viewed in this larger community context.

Fifth, park advocates need to have a future orientation. As population density and commercial development continue to exert pressure on the last remnants of open space in many communities, jurisdictions must undertake aggressive land banking initiatives while opportunities still exist to preserve land at affordable prices in appropriate locations. If communities wait until they have enough financial capacity to fully fund these purchases, the opportunities likely will have vanished. The solution, particularly in rapidly growing communities, is to issue debt that can be retired by existing and future residents and businesses.

A creative mix that includes a central downtown park, plazas, rooftop parks, promenades, entryways, trails, and street trees is vital to the revitalization and vitality of central business districts.

Sixth, park supporters need to network now more than ever. Community associations, Friends organizations, park foundations, professional associations, national and local land trusts, and other park advocates need to interact more effectively with one another and with a host of elected and appointed officials. They need to embrace modern marketing and communication disciplines, from web sites to focus groups. They need to be politically engaged and media savvy. They need to connect with and engage the general public to ensure that parks are on the public agenda.

Finally, parks will always face a funding challenge. While they have historically been viewed as a classic public good financed through general taxation, the combination of tax-cutting initiatives and stiff competition for public dollars suggests a new approach is in order. The time has come for park advocates to embrace a wider array of funding options, from the traditional to the exotic. A full menu of public, nonprofit, and private financing options exists that can and must be pursued with vigor for park systems to survive these turbulent times.

CONCLUSION

Parks matter to people. They are heavily used and dearly loved, and they deserve to be protected and appreciated by elected and appointed officials as much as they are by their users. A community needs its parks. They provide a signature for the community by contributing to its identity and personality. They provide beauty, respite, and opportunity for organized and spontaneous play. They complete the urban living experience and therefore need to be elevated to a higher priority than in the past. Above all, they need to be understood in both the historic and modern context.

While urban life has changed dramatically since the first major park sites were introduced in the U.S. more than 150 years ago, the role and purpose of parks has not changed that dramatically. In many ways, given the super-charged pace of living in the twenty-first century, parks have become even more vital than when they were the only game in town. While people today have many more leisure options than the people who lived when parks were first introduced, parks still represent perhaps the most important opportunity for users to recharge their batteries and escape the rigors and demands of urban life. Planning for parks and recognizing their significant role in the complex parks, open space, and recreation system are perhaps the best means to ensure not just their survival but their prosperity.

CHAPTER 1 REFERENCES

Cranz, Galen. 1989. *The Politics of Park Design: A History of Urban Parks in America*. Cambridge, Mass.: MIT Press.

Mertes, James D., and James R. Hall. 1996. *Park, Recreation, Open Space and Greenway Guidelines*. Washington, D.C.: National Recreation and Park Association.

Schinz, Marina and Susan Littlefield. 2002. *Visions of Paradise*. New York: Harry N. Abrams.

CHAPTER 2

Park System Functions and Services

By Mary Eysenbach

As Chapter 1 notes, a park and open space system can have many different types of elements, including the typical ones—parks, sports complexes, plazas, and tot lots—and the atypical ones—viewsheds, water trails, cemeteries, and community gardens. No matter how a community defines its park system, all of its elements have one thing in common: they are, first and foremost, *places*. In the struggle to plan and design effective park systems, that key principle is often overlooked. One primary mission of a park system is to provide recreation, an *activity* that often takes place within park systems, but recreation can also occur in other places. Conversely, activities other than recreation occur in park systems. Therefore, the terms "parks" and "recreation" are neither synonymous nor interchangeable.

During a recent visit to Bryant Park in New York City, this distinction was reinforced when I observed about one-quarter of the people in the seating areas of the park actually working: typing on their laptops, making phone calls, and even having meetings. Clearly, this is not recreation. They were there for the place that is a park. Planners engaged in planning park and open space systems must understand that fundamental distinction; it is the foundation for creating a parks and open space system that maximizes benefits for residents and other users.

THE MULTIPLE ROLES OF PARKS

As places, parks serve multiple roles. For those planning parks, this divergence matters because:

- defining a broader scope of park functions broadens citizen and leadership support for parks;
- identifying new purposes and roles for parks opens new funding streams for planning and management; and
- articulating the broader functions creates a more effective use of space and a better integrated urban environment.

Decision makers often perceive parks and recreation services as nice amenities to have but not essential community services similar to public safety and road repair. This perception means parks and recreation departments are often the hardest hit in budgetary reduction

Mary Eysenbach

Clearly, parks are places for activities other than recreation. In Bryant Park, you have people creating their own "office in nature."

measures. But it is clear parks are essential and vital elements of a healthy city and citizenry.

When the U.S. urban parks movement began, advocates marketed parks as facilities for health and social development, for uplifting people. While these proponents recognized that parks would be used during leisure hours, the purpose of parks was not solely to cater to leisure, but to provide a "natural" setting in the community to achieve larger social goals.

Current proponents of parks can use a similar approach. For instance, parks reduce stress by exposing humans to the natural world within a man-made environment, and, therefore, serve a human health function. In the Bryant Park example, while the park users were engaged in many activities, including eating, working, and recreating, they were all probably simultaneously enjoying the public health benefit of exposure to nature and other people. Similarly, when properly planned, parks can deliver environmental benefits, economic development enhancements, and even alternative transportation options, among others. By positioning parks as a means of delivering these broader benefits, advocates can find new support for placing park creation and maintenance higher on the list of essential community services deserving political and economic support. Park leaders can then approach a budget meeting with a new set of partners in tow to champion parks: health care providers, environmental groups, chambers of commerce, and bicycle and pedestrian advocates, for example.

In addition to political support, broadening the scope of park services expands the potential funding sources for parks. For instance, in recognition of the public health impacts of parks, Heart Clinic Arkansas is targeting the medical community to raise nearly $1 million in private funds to construct the "Medical Mile" section of the Arkansas River Trail in Little Rock, Arkansas. From a federal funding perspective, there's more money available for trails (as transportation) in the Federal Highway Administration (FHWA) than from the National Park Service (NPS). In the first 10 years (1992 to 2001) of the Intermodal Surface Transportation Efficiency Acts (ISTEA and TEA-21), more than $3 billion was spent on bicycle and pedestrian facilities alone. The Safe, Accountable, Flexible, Efficient Transportation Equity Act: A Legacy for Users (SAFETEA-LU), the most recent reauthorization of the acts, will make more than $4 billion available for bicycle and pedestrian projects (http://www.fhwa.dot.gov/safetealu/index.htm). In contrast, spending for the Urban Parks and Recreation Recovery Act (UPARR) between its enactment in 1978 and 2002 was $272 million. Since 2002 UPARR has received no funding. Another federal parks program, the Land and Water Conservation Fund (LWCF) distributed approximately $3.7 billion between 1965 and 2005 to states to fund open space acquisition and park development. While not all of the $7 billion for bicycle and pedestrian facilities contained in the various enactments of ISTEA are used to fund trail construction, one can see which program has greater financial resources.

By considering the broader impacts of parks, advocates from a number of public service departments can carry out their missions more efficiently through parks, making each dollar spent on each service go further. For instance, parks and open spaces can provide "green infrastructure" that supplements or replaces stormwater sewer investments while simultaneously providing passive and active recreation opportunities, which, in turn, deliver a public health service. Trails that link residential development with schools can provide safe routes for children to travel between home and school, reducing potential accidents (another public health concern) while decreasing carbon emissions from cars and buses formerly used to deliver those same children to their schools. In some cases, this kind of holistic planning occurs at the project level. To be the most effective, however, this planning must be expanded to an integrated, systemwide approach involving the community at large as well as the many municipal departments whose budgets can be stretched through effective planning.

A NEW VOCABULARY

One way to better recognize the various functions of our parks and open spaces is to change the vocabulary that describes them. Traditional park classification systems usually sort by geographic service area or size—neighborhood park versus regional park, for example. (See Table 2-1.) Those descriptions are usually further amplified with details about the park's facilities and one or two descriptions of the park's main features (e.g., the park features a sports complex or nature preserve). More recently, contemporary park

Broadening the scope of park services gains political and funding allies. Health Clinic Arkansas is raising money from the medical profession to support the Medical Mile portion of the Arkansas River Trail in Little Rock.

National Park Service, RTCA Program

TABLE 2-1. PARKS AND GREENWAYS CLASSIFICATIONS

CLASSIFICATION	GENERAL DESCRIPTION	SIZE AND SERVICE AREA CRITERIA
NEIGHBORHOOD PARK	Neighborhood parks are the basic units of the park system and serve a recreational and social purpose. Focus is on informal recreation.	Typically 5 acres or more, 8 to 10 acres preferred, with 3 acres the desired minimum size. Service area is ¼ to ½ mile uninterrupted by major roads and other physical barriers.
COMMUNITY PARK	Serves a broader purpose than neighborhood parks. Focus is on meeting community-based recreational needs, as well as preserving unique landscapes and open spaces.	Varies, depending on function. A minimum of 20 acres is preferred, with 40 or more acres optimal. Service area can be communitywide or several neighborhoods in given area of the community.
LARGE URBAN PARK	Large urban parks are generally associated with larger urban centers with large populations. Focus is on meeting wide-ranging community needs and preserving unique and sometimes extensive landscapes and open spaces.	Varies depending on circumstances. A typical minimum size is 50 acres, with hundreds of acres not uncommon, such as Central Park in New York City.
YOUTH ATHLETIC COMPLEX/FACILITY	Consolidates programmed youth athletic fields and associated facilities to fewer strategically located sites throughout the community. Also can provide some neighborhood use functions.	Varies, with 20 acres or more desirable, but not absolute. Optimal size is 40 to 80 acres.
COMMUNITY ATHLETIC COMPLEX/FACILITY	Consolidates programmed adult and youth athletic fields and associated facilities to a limited number of sites. Tournament level facilities are appropriate.	Varies, with 20 acres or more desirable, but not absolute. Optimal size is 40 to 80 acres.
GREENWAY	Lands set aside for preserving natural resources, remnant landscapes, and open space, and providing visual aesthetics/buffering. Also provides passive use opportunities. Ecological resource stewardship and wildlife protection are high priorities. Suitable for ecologically sensitive trail corridors.	Varies, depending on opportunity and general character of natural systems within the community.
PARKWAY	Linear park-like transportation corridors between public parks, monuments, institutions, and sometimes business centers. Can be maintained green space or natural in character.	Varies.
SPECIAL USE	Covers a broad range of parks and recreation facilities oriented toward single-purpose uses, such as a nature center, historic sites, plazas, urban squares, aquatic centers, campgrounds, and golf courses.	Varies, depending on need.
PARK-SCHOOL	School sites that are used in concert with, or in lieu of, other types of parks to meet community park and recreation needs. School sites often provide the majority of indoor recreational facilities within a community.	Varies, depending on specific site opportunities.
PRIVATE PARK/ RECREATION FACILITY	Parks and recreation facilities that are privately owned, yet contribute to the public park and recreation system.	Varies.
REGIONAL PARKS AND PARK RESERVES	Larger scale, regionally based parks and open spaces that focus on natural resource preservation and stewardship.	Typically a minimum of 500 acres and up to several thousand. Service area is regional, which generally encompasses several cities.

researchers have conceptualized alternative ways to classify parks in ways that better describe the role of the modern park in the community and its relation to its users and community residents.

In 1989, Patrik Grahn, a Swedish landscape architect, used a survey of park users to classify parks according to the way they characterized the park and its function. Table 2-2 shows the results.

Grahn's classification emphasizes function over facilities. It also introduces a broader role for parks. Species-rich and plaza parks function as educational places, while festive ones develop social capital.

One of the most unusual innovations in park vocabulary is "harlequin space." Created by British landscape architect Tom Turner, this term ascribes moods and the colors associated with them to park spaces. For instance, "red" parks generate a mood of excitement and unpredictability. "Brown" parks are wholesome and earthy. Turner also urges the use of functional terms for parks. Referring to the cooling effect of green areas, he calls these places "air-conditioning parks," and parks that provide stormwater storage are "flood parks." He calls for "ethnic parks" to retain the outdoor traditions of various groups and "art parks" to work synergistically with galleries to spread art out into the community.

While Turner's color approach may seem more suited for a studio design exercise than practical typology, it does advance the notion of parks as places by focusing on user experience and emotion, rather than activities. His second approach, naming parks according to function, helps broaden the role of parks. Realistically, however, most parks provide multiple services. A park employed for stormwater storage may also be providing air-conditioning (and maybe species habitat, fitness trails, and perhaps, a tourism attraction). It would be cumbersome to ascribe names based on all of those services.

A similar quandary exists when trying to sort different functions into categories. Park benefits are typically divided into groups, such as social, economic, or environmental benefits. In practice, however, these benefits overlap among groups. For instance, reducing the urban heat island effect (that is, the phenomenon of higher temperatures in urban areas caused by heat absorbed by asphalt, concrete, and other similar surfaces) is an environmental benefit and also positively affects public health by providing cooling and even energy savings by reducing air-conditioning needs. And all these functions have economic implications (e.g., reductions in overall air-conditioning use) although we may not be able to measure them precisely.

TABLE 2-2. PARK CLASSIFICATIONS BY FUNCTION

1. Wilderness park: hiking and camping
2. Species-rich park: observing, collecting species
3. Forest park: physical culture, running
4. Play park: play equipment, building, growing
5. Sports park: arena sports
6. Peaceful park: garden studies, games for fun
7. Festive park: social meetings, togetherness
8. Plaza park: architectural study, garden study

Source: Grahn 1990.

To capture this concept of the multiple purposes of parks, I have organized their services into the following categories:

- Civic and Social Capital
- Cultural Expression
- Economic Development
- Education
- Green Infrastructure
- Public Health
- Recreation
- Urban Form

These functions reflect some of the more common services parks and open space elements provide their communities, but this list is by no means complete. Park planners must interview community residents and observe how sites are used to accurately identify these functions in their communities. Changing demographics, cultural shifts, and physical changes to sites, neighborhoods, and the city itself can all alter the way residents perceive parks and their public as well as "natural" function.

Mary Eysenbach

Parks are the embodiment of democracy. People can, and do, appear in parks to speak to their fellow citizens about what is on their minds.

Civic and Social Capital

Parks connect people to each other. They reflect the great melting pot of American society, where people gather regardless of income, ethnicity, age, or profession. Although different cultures perceive and use open space differently, parks are democratic spaces. People from all walks of life gather and mingle in public parks. And because anyone can be in the park, the park experience is virtually guaranteed to be new with each visit. While parks are thought of as places to "get away" from it all, that "all" does not usually include other people. Research conducted at wilderness areas and national parks demonstrates that in these large areas most people gravitate to where other people are. As public gathering spaces, parks are critical social and civic spaces because they are the places where we assemble to express our democratic rights, join together to express collective emotion, meet our neighbors, and establish a sense of belonging.

Freedom space. Parks are the embodiment of democracy. Ideally, all people are equal there, and each person may speak his mind. Large protests may march in the street, but when it comes to the speech making, the destination is usually a public park or square. This space is integral to the architecture of democracy. In great cities, some of these spaces are typically in the center of the city or adjacent to the buildings where government resides. In London, Hyde Park's Speaker's Corner is an icon of free speech and thought, hosting both famous and common citizens in a space specifically for expressing opinion.

Celebration and solace. By providing space for large numbers of people, and as places where we connect as a citizenry, parks are sites of collective joy. Whether it is an annual event, such as Fourth of July fireworks, or a singular event, such as winning a World Series title or the Stanley Cup, parks are often the places we gather to celebrate. Similarly, a shared devastating event sends people to these public spaces to grieve collectively. Washington Square and Union Square in New York City became places for temporary memorials following September 11, 2001. Parks are also typically the setting for permanent memorials, from the World War II remembrances that grace nearly every public park system in the U.S., to the Strawberry Fields peace garden in Central Park, to the Vietnam War Memorial on The Mall in Washington, D.C.

"Third places." Third places are locations, apart from home ("first") and work ("second"), where people seek community. Although we sometimes tend to think of third places as commercial establishments (the corner coffee shop), neighborhood parks also play this role. A Chicago public housing study revealed that residents with access to proximate green space engaged more frequently in social activities, have more visitors, know more of their neighbors, and have stronger feelings of belonging (Kuo 1998). The research showed that the attractiveness of grass and trees in common spaces drew residents to them, fostering casual social interactions. In addition to attractive vegetation, parks may provide particular facilities that attract people and provide social interaction. For instance, mothers may use a playground as a meeting place, or dog owners gather with other owners at a neighborhood park specifically designed for dog owners' use. In order for a park to truly generate "third place" benefits (such as a sense of belonging, community, and safety), it is better that it be located within walking distance for users (Oldenburg 1996). When considering how a park system works as a third place, planners need to understand how the individual components of the system (that is, the specific facilities assigned to parks and the "reach" of the

Mary Eysenbach

We go to parks to celebrate and to remember, whether it be to cheer at a parade for a local sports championship team or to place a wreath of flowers at a memorial to those who gave their lives for cause and country.

park) provide these benefits (for example, by considering the demographics of the area—elderly, young singles with dogs, or high concentration of families).

Branding. A park can give a community an identity. Think of all the neighborhood names that include the word "park." Think of all the businesses close to parks that contain the park's name. What a park looks like, and how it functions, can be a positive—or negative—reflection of a community's self-definition. When a community strongly identifies with the park, local park revitalization can spark community revitalization. On a citywide scale, park restorations, like Central Park in New York, or new parks, like Millennium Park in Chicago, create vibrancy and esteem.

Government by the people. Parks are an excellent tool for civic engagement. Self-determination, through park planning participation, can spread to other community issues. Parks are particularly suited to encourage participation because their scale, in most cases, makes it easy for community residents to become engaged (the concern is usually quite "local") and, given the way a park is used or, conversely, not used by residents provides a focal point for discussion. It is rare that specific park-related issues are complicated by policy issues or multiyear timelines. People may feel that parks provide an opportunity to be heard in a way that is far more "hands-on" than usual. This exposure to civic engagement, especially and most importantly if it results in successful change, can be a gateway to further community activity by participants.

Cultural Expression

Closely aligned with the social and civic functions of parks are functions that support cultural heritage. Parks can be the venues for any number of cultural displays, including: performance arts, such as dance, music, and theatre; public art, be it temporary or permanent installations; and special events. In conjunction with their capacity to gather people together, parks

Millennium Park in Chicago is a 24.5-acre "open house" of art and interactive art features. It also includes a music pavilion designed by Frank Gehry for public performances.

Mary Eysenbach

are "festival" places (Harvest Fest, Greek Fest, Taste of Yourcityhere, etc.). Parks are often home to community museums. Some parks contain important historical buildings or artifacts, or they are historical places themselves. Likewise, a park, by virtue of its design or designer, is itself "art."

Song and dance. From the quintessential brass band concert in the park gazebo to Shakespeare in the Park performances throughout the summer season, parks have historically hosted live performances. Increasingly, cities are planning and designing these spaces with performance in mind. Some are building state-of-the-art band shells with high-tech sound systems. Others simply create slopes and arrange seating to accommodate performances without the need for high-tech facilities.

Like the presence parks have given to musical and dramatic performance, they have also given a presence to public art. Public art has a long history in parks, from the sculptures that dot public squares in Europe to the efforts of the Works Project Administration (WPA) to relieve unemployment after the Depression to create distinctive places commemorating history and

Seattle Parks and Recreation Department

Parks can put design on display. Freeway Park in Seattle is one of several in the U.S. built over a local highway. As noted in Chapter 5 of this PAS Report, creative partnerships with unlikely partners, like the transportation department, can also help put parks where none might have thought they could exist.

civic pride. Today, parks are home to a wide range of art installations, from permanent sculptures like those found in the Minneapolis Sculpture Garden to temporary exhibits, such as Central Park's 2005 exhibition of "The Gates." In Chicago, the 24.5-acre Millennium Park is basically an outdoor gallery of interactive art and architectural installations, including the "Cloudgate" sculpture by Anish Kapoor and the Jay Pritzker Music Pavilion by Frank Gehry, which marries public art with music performance.

Celebrating identity. Most major cities have some sort of festival meant to express cultural identity or uniqueness. These festivals include a wide range of events, such as ethnic pride celebrations, religious holidays, and "taste of . . . " events. These cultural expressions take place in neighborhood parks and larger, central business district parks, the latter often designed to accommodate large crowds. Like special performance spaces, cities are increasingly cognizant of the need for a large festival space and its concomitant design demands.

Mary Eysenbach

Historic parks can memorialize a number of events. Point State Park in Pittsburgh is located on the former site of Fort Pitt, a 1758 fort built during the French and Indian War. Today, the Point serves as a key green space for the city's cultural and special events.

In Los Angeles, the newest park in the city, Cornfield State Park, is ideally situated to embrace the fullness of its ethnic identity. It is located in the heart of L.A. in a neighborhood that has received many of the immigrants who arrived in America beginning in the late eighteenth century. In its plan for the park, the California State Park Advisory Committee recommended that the site "embrace the spirit and hopes of the multi-ethnic communities whose histories and struggles are interwoven with the Cornfield. . . . Historical and cultural narratives can enrich common activities of the site—recreation, education, and interpretation—and can serve to inspire and engender cultural connections" (Cornfield 2003).

Cultural institution support. Parks often host community cultural institutions. Museums of natural history, science, and art are found in major parks around the world and, in some cases, are even subsidized by the parks department. In addition to these larger institutions, partnerships between parks departments and smaller galleries, performance companies, libraries, and even artist-in-residence programs serve to make parks the places for cultural expression.

Preserving history. Some of the most important cultural resources located in parks are historical ones. The historical resource might be a building. Often, the land may have been the location of an historical event, or, in the case of an archaeological site, a historic period. In these cases, the site is likely to be publicly owned and managed as a park in order to protect it from development. On occasion, a park may preserve a historic vernacular landscape rather than the site of an event. For instance, the Ohio & Erie National Heritage Canalway is a regional project that preserves the landscape of those historic canals. In conjunction with the heritage effort, local park departments have developed a trail along the towpath, combining exercise, education, and civic pride.

A park, by virtue of its design or designer, can also be an important historic resource. Like buildings, park landscapes by famous designers, such as Fredrick Law Olmsted, or parks that significantly reflect a design innovation, such as Freeway Park in Seattle, help provide insight into the urban and architectural philosophies and movements that have influenced urban development.

The art of landscape. Parks have an aesthetic function. Across cultural lines, certain landscape preferences and characteristics prevail (consider the differences between English, French, and American parks and their design and maintenance). People generally find beauty in nature, especially when it has been arranged into a legible form for them. Park landscapes, therefore, are, in essence, a form of public art.

Economic Development

The idea is rather simple: plan a park or green space where people want to be, manage it well, and they will come. And generally, they bring money to spend on housing, goods, and services. The economic benefits following that attraction depend upon the forms and locations of the parks. A well-planned and managed park system enhances residential real estate values adjacent to parks, improves retail and commercial values, and helps draw and retain tourists, retirees, and an educated workforce.

Location, location, location. In the U.S., one of the most prominent examples of these economic benefits is Fredrick Law Olmsted's demonstration that Central Park in New York more than repaid the public dollars used for its development through the increase in proximate property values and real estate taxes. In 2001, a review of 25 studies conducted before 1990 to assess the impact of a park on adjacent real estate found that parks and open space positively affected property values in 20 of those studies (Crompton 2001).

The trend continues today. Recent reviews of the literature on parks and real estate values found that neighborhood parks may provide up to a 20 percent increase in housing values for homes facing the park, with the proximity benefit extending approximately 600 to 800 feet (Nicholls 2004). Larger community parks may provide benefits up to a 33 percent increase in the residential real estate value, with the positive effect extending as far as 2,000 feet (Economic Research Associates 2005). These effects are contingent upon a number of variables, including level of park maintenance, visibility of the park, noise and street congestion generated by park users, and even the landscape itself.

Some parks are serving economic development ends as well as providing space to re-create. Pioneer Courthouse Square in Portland, Oregon, acts as an "anchor tenant" for surrounding retailers and does it quite successfully.

Courtesy of Duane Morris Photography & Pioneer Courthouse Square

Even in the absence of research data, one needs to look only at the private real estate development market to assess the importance of parks and open space to value. While many real estate developments are required, by ordinance, to provide open space, developers find that providing such space pays off both in the short and long runs. A quick survey of the real estate section in any Sunday newspaper demonstrates that residential builders are likely to tout their developments' easy access to parks, "parklike" settings, or park or preserve views within the advertising copy or graphic representation of the project. In these cases, parks are clearly a desired amenity that helps the market the development.

Parks as anchor tenants. The renovation of Bryant Park in New York City stands as the poster child for using a well-designed and managed park to positively influence the surrounding area. Occupancy rates and rents rose in the surrounding buildings, confirming for those owners that their decision to pay a special assessment for the park was money well spent. Many other cities have followed suit. Chattanooga and Pittsburgh revitalized their riverfronts. Cleveland and Atlanta focused on central business district sites. All are key components of an urban design scheme where, as Grover Mouton, III, director of Tulane's Regional Urban Design Center observed at the City Park Forum meeting in Reno, Nevada, in 2002, "parks . . . become real anchor tenants if you look at them correctly." For example, Portland's Pioneer Square is a 1.56-acre site that combines a programmed public plaza with a public transit station, bringing throngs of people to the location. "It's no wonder that retailers clamber to anchor their stores within a few blocks of the sprawling square. Nordstrom, Banana Republic, Gap, Meier & Frank, and Abercrombie & Fitch all border the square . . . " (Stout 2001).

Disneylike. Whereas the effect of parks on proximate residential and commercial property values is largely site specific, the ability of parks to draw tourists, an educated workforce, and retirees occurs on a city or regional scale. The original theme—build it and they will come (with money in their pockets)—still holds. For instance, tourism is driven by attractions, many of which the public park system or nonprofit organizations in partnership with the public system, provide (Crompton 2002). Jon B. DeVries, founding director of the Chicago School of Real Estate at Roosevelt University, estimates that Chicago's recently opened Millennium Park, which has between 3 million and 4.4 million visitors annually, increases annual hotel earnings by $42 million to $58 million, restaurant earnings by $67 million to $87 million, and retail earnings by $53 million to $71 million (Uhlir 2006).

Attracting Generation X, Y, & ?. With the growth of footloose businesses in the technical and service sectors, cities have begun to understand the importance of improving the quality of life to attract and retain employers and employees. One reason is that employers need educated and creative employees. A 2006 survey conducted for the group, CEOs for Cities, reveals that two-thirds of highly mobile 25- to 34-year-olds with college degrees say they will decide where they live first, then look for a job (Cortright 2005). These coveted employees value place and quality of life amenities. Among typical place amenities, such as beauty and access to recreation, park systems have much to contribute to attracting employees of the changing economy.

Attracting Baby Boomers. While economic development research has given greater weight to the quality of life in a place as a factor in determining what kind of workforce a community can attract and retain, it is also the case that quality of life, including access to parks and open space, is a primary concern for retirees with sufficient income to afford to move to such a place. The image of retirees following the sun and warm weather is older than Sun City in Arizona. And like Sun City and even cold climate retirement developments, communities that provide amenities supporting these seniors' active lifestyles will be successful in capturing their share of the retirement migration. The importance of attracting this growing demographic and its steady, sizable assets has led many communities to establish programs directed at attracting the retirees.

Quality of life, including access to parks and open space, is a primary concern for retirees with sufficient income to afford to move to such a place.

Education

Parks can serve as important educational resources in a community, both as additions to school campuses and as stand-alone facilities. The lessons learned from parks, for both children and adults, range from biology to civics.

Weeding and writing. Many cities have embarked on a campaign to replace their schools' asphalt surroundings with campus parks. These campus parks may be expanses of turf and trees for unstructured play or the site for game facilities. Some campus parks contain natural plantings and native nature areas to enhance classroom curriculum. The Washington Elementary School in Berkeley, California, has replaced a 1.5-acre barren asphalt yard with the Environmental Yard, a series of mini-ecosystems reflecting the region. Play structures and community gathering areas have transformed the schoolyard into a year-round, seven-day-a-week, educational resource (Moore 2003).

Learning naturally. Parks need not be physically connected to schools to be places of learning. Most environmental education centers, as well as zoological and botanical gardens, are located in parks. They typically have extensive educational programs for adults and children. Beyond these structured facilities, children love to explore informal natural park areas. They acquire valuable skills in concentration, creativity, and motor coordination through these encounters (Chawla and Cushing 2007). In fact, a 1998 study showed the positive impact of using off-site open spaces to expand the learning resources on the standardized achievement scores of socially disadvantaged students (Lieberman and Hoody 1998). Another learning opportunity arises when citizens, both children and adults, participate in the planning of parks. Participants learn about cooperation, democracy, design, and advocacy. These exercises can expand upon civic lessons learned in classrooms.

Green Infrastructure

Green infrastructure refers to urban landscapes that perform environmental work, such as cleaning air and runoff, restoring groundwater, maintaining the native plant gene pool, and providing wildlife habitat (Girling 2005). In the case of parks, it reflects the services provided by natural features that would otherwise be delivered by "gray" infrastructure, such as storm sewer facilities and pollution mitigation systems.

Trees and native plantings absorb carbon dioxide and serve as pollutant sinks to clean the air. Green spaces also help keep urban areas cooler.

Parks also indirectly play a positive function in human health through the environmental services provided by pervious surfaces and vegetative cover. Unpaved surfaces absorb stormwater, helping to improve the water quality of surface water and groundwater resources. Trees and native plantings absorb carbon dioxide and serve as pollutant sinks to clean the air. Green spaces also help keep urban areas cooler. In conjunction with linear parks and greenways, trails can serve as transportation corridors, reducing the pressure for roadway expansion and roadway congestion. And by protecting and restoring the ecological integrity of areas, parks and open spaces can help preserve biological diversity.

Drink up. It pays to invest in preserving land to protect the water we eventually drink. New York City, for instance, anticipated this value when it began to purchase land in upstate New York to protect the water quality of the reservoirs that provide the city's water supply. A recent World Bank analysis estimates this preservation strategy is seven times cheaper than building and operating a treatment plant; that figure reflects only capital investment, not the annual cost to operate the plant; in other words, it's even a better deal than it looks (Dudley 2003).

Unlike New York's surface water source, San Antonio is dependent upon water from below ground—the Edwards Aquifer. Here, city officials have embarked on an open space protection program that directs development downstream from the aquifer's recharge zones. In May 2000, San Antonio residents approved the "aquifer" tax, a one-eighth-cent sales tax, to purchase undeveloped land in the recharge zone.

California's Proposition 84, passed in 2006, gives the state the ability to issue bonds worth more than $5 billion to fund projects related to safe drinking water, water quality and supply, flood control, waterway and natural resource protection, water pollution and contamination control, water conservation efforts, park improvements, and public access to natural resources (Attorney General of California 2006). In this case, the funding will not focus on human-made interventions, such as dams and water storage facilities, but on protecting the water sources themselves. As is clear from the list of options that will be employed to accomplish this goal, parks and open space will play a major role.

Many cities create synergistic systems between their parks and water reservoirs. Not only does the open space protect natural water supplies, it can provide environmental education and recreation opportunities. Even in cases where a reservoir is part of a gray infrastructure system, the reservoirs serve as water features within park sites. More recently, due to water supply safety concerns, cities have capped their reservoirs and created usable open space on top of the caps.

Even recreation surfaces can be more ecologically friendly as Philadelphia proved by building basketball courts with pervious surfaces: water runs through into an underground storage space where it can be drawn off gradually, and the court dries faster.

Philadelphia Water Department

Holding back the waters. In addition to protecting drinking water, parks and open spaces can deliver critical stormwater management services. On- and off-site mitigation projects can create attractive, functional additions to existing parks sites or create entirely new parks. Many of the best management practices used in reducing runoff are ideally suited for parks and open space. For instance, vegetative swales use bio-infiltration to intercept and slow runoff. These plantings are ideal treatments within parks to mitigate impervious surfaces, such as parking lots and roadways. Park trees also help reduce runoff by intercepting rainfall and absorbing precipitation. In California, TreePeople has developed a program called T.R.E.E.S. (Transagency Resources for Economic and Environmental Sustainability) to demonstrate the value of urban trees in stormwater management. Participants include the U.S. Environmental Protection Agency, the cities of Los Angeles and Santa Monica, the Los Angeles County Department of Public Works, the Metropolitan Water District, and the Southern California Association of Governments (Urban Forest Ecosystems Institute n.d.).

Other examples of park systems serving a water storage function include the following:

- Water utility and park planners are working together to improve the storage capacity of existing parks by restoring habitat along streams.

- In Philadelphia, the installation of pervious basketball court surfaces has a dual benefit: water filters through the pores in the surface into an underground storage bed, while the same pores allow the court to dry faster after a rain (Coutts 2006).

- Wet and dry basins can be designed within park settings to create water features and wetlands, such as the Orlando, Florida, Greenwood Urban Wetland Park, a 19-acre site with attractive plantings, walkways, bridges, and benches that functions as a stormwater treatment facility.

One cautionary note here: while stormwater basins are great partners in parks, the use of basin acreage to satisfy mandatory recreational open space dedication requirements is controversial. Land that is wet a significant portion of the year will not be available for many typical recreational uses.

Cool. In addition to providing clean water, parks and their vegetation can help clean and cool the air. Parks and open spaces are critical components in a city's urban forest. Trees absorb harmful gases, such as sulfur dioxide, carbon monoxide, and ozone. Research conducted by American Forests in 1996 estimated that Atlanta's tree cover removed 19 million pounds of pollutants each year. When that total was multiplied by externality costs (costs to society not reflected in the marketplace), the value of the tree cover was estimated at $47 million. In addition to filtering pollutants, trees trap and store carbon, a key contributor to global climate change.

Speaking of warming, parks can help reduce the urban heat island effect. The Center for Urban Horticulture at the University of Washington estimates that a mature tree canopy can reduce air temperature by 5 to 10 degrees through shade and transpiration. In addition to trees, the open spaces in parks create a "park cool island effect" (Spronken-Smith 1999). Spin-off benefits from the lower temperatures include a reduction in ozone, plus fewer pollutants generated by technologies used to provide air conditioning. These improvements add up. The Atlanta study cited above also attributed $2.8 million in energy savings. Coupled with their ability to sequester carbon, trees and vegetative air-conditioning will grow in importance as the planet faces even greater climate change. One of the strategies under consideration by the Japanese environmental ministry to mitigate the urban heat island effect is to design a network of interconnected green spaces and water to ensure wind flow (Ministry of the Environment, Government of Japan 2004).

Getting around. A critical (and expensive) component of any urban infrastructure is transportation. The relationship between transportation and parks was in evidence early in the U.S. when park planners, like Olmsted, created boulevards to extend the reach of parks. They accomplished this by adding a wide strip of landscaped open space that either separated lanes of traffic or separated faster moving traffic lanes from slower, parallel frontage streets. By creating a vegetated "route" by which people could access their larger parks, they also shortened the distance by which many citizens could access green space. Other green spaces that run contiguous with streets, such as parkways or New Orleans' "neutral grounds" can, depending upon width, have long-served as neighborhood open space.

The primary focus of mobility planning, of course, is still mobility for the automobile. That may be changing, however. Rising obesity rates and the political, economic, and environmental problems caused by our reliance on fossil fuels are demanding that communities plan transportation infrastructure to accommodate other modes of transportation equally or in preference

One of the strategies under consideration by the Japanese environmental ministry to mitigate the urban heat island effect is to design a network of interconnected green spaces and water to ensure wind flow.

to gasoline-powered vehicles. With funding assistance from ISTEA, TEA-21, and SAFETY-LU, communities are building bike and pedestrian paths within parks, greenways, and other open space corridors to provide alternative forms of transportation.

In some cases, planners are taking advantage of transportation corridors to create linear parks that contain trail systems. In Boston, public objection to the expansion of I-95 during the late 1960s prompted the governor to stop the highway project. An analysis of alternatives and public participation pointed to the need for public transportation and community revitalization for an area laid bare by the demolition done to prepare for highway construction. In a bold move, the governor transferred both the land and construction funding to serve transit as well as community development. Today, high-speed Amtrak and local commuter rail lines run below grade, and at ground level, a linear park in the tradition of Olmsted's Emerald Necklace links Arnold Arboretum and Franklin Park with downtown Boston near the Fenway.

Charlotte/Mecklenburg County, North Carolina, has undertaken a 16.5-mile greenway project to control flooding along Little Sugar Creek, which receives the city of Charlotte's runoff. Flood areas, like those shown in the upper-right photo, have been converted to parks like those in the larger photo.

Charlotte/Mecklenburg Parks and Recreation

Biodiversity. In addition to parks and open spaces functioning as substitutes for gray infrastructure, they can also provide infrastructure that promotes and preserves biodiversity. Biodiversity is the variety of all the genes, species, and ecosystems found within a defined area. The green infrastructure benefits described above depend upon biodiversity, as does human life itself.

In developed areas in and around cities, parks and open spaces are key components of biodiversity. Though they are rarely home to the large reserves that support large numbers of different species or large populations of one species, local parks can protect rare microhabitats and remnants of matrix habitat for generalist species (Perlman 2005). Depending on their location, width, and human use, greenways can serve as both habitat for edge species (those plants and animals that thrive along the borders of environments), as well as wildlife corridors, allowing passage for wildlife while eliminating the danger to both passenger traffic and animals.

The greatest potential for parks and open space to preserve biodiversity lies in a communal effort by parks and open space agencies to plan land acquisition, development, and management. This approach is exemplified by Chicago Wilderness, a consortium of public agencies, nonprofit organizations and educational institutions dedicated to preserving and restoring the natural ecosystems of Chicago. Although it seems incredible, the more than 225,000 acres of land held by Chicago Wilderness's members contain the largest concentration of endangered and threatened species in the Midwest. These native communities are more threatened than those in the tropical rainforests (Shore 1997). But as is true in most developed metropolitan regions, the biodiversity resides in a mosaic of remnant natural areas where the links and other necessary elements that would promote greater safety and preservation are sometimes missing. The best hope for maintaining this biodiversity is the alliance and cooperation of more than 180 public and private organizations to join, preserve, and manage the pieces of that mosaic.

Disaster-proofing. A more unusual infrastructure function of parks and open space is hazard mitigation. By planning parks and open space in areas where development might be threatened by landslides, wildfires, earthquakes, or floods, communities can minimize the life and property destruction caused by natural hazards by placing open space, not human beings, in the danger zones. In addition, the services provided by open spaces can help prevent or minimize damage to adjacent areas. For instance, trees help hold soil on hillsides, protecting downslope areas. Open areas between forests and developments can be wildfire buffers.

The most frequent use of green space for preventing hazard damage is for flood mitigation. By reserving the land next to rivers and streams as open space, communities create flood-storage areas for themselves and for communities downstream. Charlotte/Mecklenburg County, North Carolina, for example, has embarked on a 16.5-mile urban greenway project to control flooding along Little Sugar Creek, the prime recipient of Charlotte's runoff.

Public Health

Fredrick Law Olmsted, whose experience as head of the Sanitary Commission during the Civil War provided him with insight into public health matters, intuitively understood the influence of parks on public health. Observing the success of Central Park, he concluded, "The lives of women and children too poor to be sent to the country can now be saved in thousands of instances by making them go to the Park. During a hot day in July last, I counted . . . eighteen separate groups, consisting of mothers with their children . . . taking picnic dinners which they had brought from home with them. The practice is increasing under medical advice, especially when summer complaint is rife" (Beveridge and Hoffman 1997).

While his musings might seem overblown to today's world of climate-controlled environments, parks continue to play a significant role in the health of urban residents. This influence falls into three main categories: encouraging physical activity, providing people contact with nature and each other, and improving environmental quality that, ultimately, affects health.

Move it. The headlines are full of statistics about the growing U.S. obesity crisis. Along with obesity, of course, comes a host of associated diseases: hypertension, diabetes, and heightened cholesterol levels. Most alarming is the number of overweight or obese children. While this trend is attributable to a number of lifestyle and cultural changes, one of the main contributing factors is a lack of physical activity. To that end, parks can serve as key health facilities in neighborhoods. This impact is especially important for older adults and children, two groups whose access to recreational facilities may

DuPage County FPD

One must not forget the recreational benefits of parks, especially in an era when obesity is a continuing problem for much of the public, especially children, both in the U.S. and elsewhere. Parks create opportunities to go out for a jog or walk (above) or to climb a tree (below), and usually without having to pay a fee as one would in a club.

Mary Eysenbach

be restricted. This impact is important also for lower-income neighborhoods whose residents often cannot afford health club memberships.

Simply providing the opportunity to exercise can increase the activity of nearby residents. A study by St. Louis University's Department of Public Health showed that, where walking trails had been built, nearly 40 percent of people with access had used the trails, and more than 55 percent of trail walkers had increased their walking since beginning to use the trails (Brownson et al. 2000). A study documented in Frumkin (2003) demonstrated that, if you build parks a certain way, the public is more likely to come; specifically, if a park is close and accessible with good lighting, well-maintained paths, toilets, drinking water, and attractive scenery, it is more likely to be used. For those people who are already physically active, mere contact with a natural setting can help enhance the benefits of exercise (Bodin and Hartig 2003).

Vitamin N(ature). The results of Bodin and Hartig's study (2003) come as no surprise to those who work in the field of ecopsychology. Even absent the physical activity, parks can bring about positive physiological and psychological effects. One reason for these benefits may be that humans are hard-wired to relate to other living things—because our evolutionary success depended upon them. The term "biophilia" describes this phenomenon and explains why humans are drawn to flowers and prefer to live near water (Wilson 1984).

Whether or not it is a genetic trait, studies show that contact with nature reduces people's stress levels. By reducing the mental fatigue associated with overstimulation, exposure to a natural setting reduces the demand for constant directed attention (trying to concentrate while distracted). That, in turn, reduces irritability, frustration, tension, and stress. It gives the mind an opportunity to recover (Kaplan and Kaplan 1998).

These psychological benefits have physiological results. Research shows that simply viewing nature can help people heal faster (Ulrich 1984). An easy way to test the relationship of nature to stress reduction: Ask a roomful of people to close their eyes and picture the most relaxing place they can imagine—a place where they are happy and peaceful. After a few minutes,

PASSIVE IS PASSÉ

The description of parks as either "passive" or "active" must be discontinued. "Passive" is a loaded term. A quick thesaurus search for synonyms yields: apathetic, flat, indifferent, inert, lifeless, resigned, sleepy, submissive, and unassertive. This is no way to describe a park and hope to gain any kind of support for it. Second, it's inaccurate. Many passive parks have very active users. Picnicking, an activity frequently identified as one for a passive park, can involve Frisbee-throwing, a pick-up softball game, badminton, or any number of pastimes requiring vigorous movement.

Upon closer examination, the two terms are typically used to describe the level of developed facilities or the level of structure that exists. "Active" parks typically have dedicated ball fields, some type of courts, or maybe a playground. The built facilities prescribe the uses of the site. In addition, these parks may be programmed with activities and staff. A passive park is usually absent any structured prescription for use. A few amenities may exist, such as a path, benches, an expanse of turf, and perhaps

a garden. The uses of the space are constrained mostly by size and surrounding uses.

Even "open space" can convey, to some, an opportunity for development, be it a highway or community center. That is not surprising, considering that a typical definition for parks within land-use classification systems is that of "undeveloped land." Again, this may give an impression that the park or space is simply in limbo until it meets its ultimate destiny as something "developed."

We need new terms to better reflect parks as places. Descriptions such as "structured" or "flexible" would better capture the design and use intent for sites. If "active" is to be used, "passive" should be replaced with "creative" or "informal" space. There is no need to define by dichotomy. In fact, whenever possible, identify parks according to their primary functions. This approach would likely boost the status of (at least some) parks by ascribing meaning to all open spaces, removing them from the inventory of "undeveloped" or "underdeveloped" land.

ask for a show of hands of how many people imagined a place where they were surrounded by natural elements, such as a beach or a garden. With a few exceptions, most will have visualized a nature place.

Recreation

Recreation is, of course, an important function of parks. The connection between parks and recreation facilities developed in earnest during the playground movement of the 1920s and has grown since then. The function of recreation in parks is delivered through three main areas: parks spaces that provide opportunities for informal or spontaneous recreational activities, recreational facilities developed for specific activities, and programs provided by recreation staff on park sites.

Informal space. The earliest parks in this country were designed with an abundance of space for informal activities. The great lawns and tree groves had aesthetic purposes, but they also encouraged park visitors to play spontaneously. While less prevalent today, many communities are recognizing the importance of these multi-use spaces. Where residential surveys once pointed to a demand for developed facilities, many citizens now express a preference for flexible spaces. An open expanse of lawn can be a place for a pick-up soccer game, a weekend block party, or seating for an evening band concert.

Structured activities. Developed recreational facilities are the most common recreation function of parks. Baseball fields, tennis courts, recreation centers, skate parks . . . the list is endless. These special facilities provide places for formal recreational activities. The park standards on which some park and open space plans are based (e.g., four acres per 1,000 population) come from a determination of the number of facilities needed by residents and then a calculation of the number of acres necessary to provide the facilities. In some cases, facilities such as ball fields are conglomerated into one location, creating a sports complex. This technique helps those managing the facility by centralizing operations and addressing community concerns about the noise and traffic that usually accompany these kinds of facilities. In other cases, these recreational facilities are distributed among neighborhood and community parks. Such dispersion can be beneficial because it makes facilities more accessible to users. Care must be taken, however, so that these facilities are not concentrated in a way that makes access and use (the positive side of such facilities) and the noise and traffic (the negative side) unequal among different populations.

Program places. In many communities, parks are the venues for recreational programming. This effort can be permanent, such as activities that take place in recreation centers located in parks or the sports leagues that organize around and use athletic facilities. Programming can also be temporary or sporadic, such as an arts performance that tours the park system or a two-week basketball camp. These programs are most often provided by the parks and recreation department, but the role of private and nonprofit partners in this endeavor is growing. For instance, the above-mentioned arts performance tour might be delivered by a local theatre or dance troupe, while the basketball camp is a result of a partnership between the city and a professional or college team. Increasingly, providing programs in parks is used to increase safety (or the perception of safety) in underused parks. It can also be an effective tool to generate attendance for new parks.

Urban Form

One of the most important functions of parks, and one that is often absent in parks and open space plans, is their role in shaping urban form. As *open* space, like negative space in painting or sculpture, parks and natural spaces

Where residential surveys once pointed to a demand for developed facilities, many citizens now express a preference for flexible spaces. An open expanse of lawn can be a place for a pick-up soccer game, a weekend block party, or seating for an evening band concert.

provide valuable counterbalance to urban landscapes. In order to most effectively deliver the multiple benefits described throughout this chapter and PAS report, park and open space systems should be planned in advance of or in light of other community development. Of course, most communities do not have a blank canvas on which to paint this preliminary green pattern. Many urban and suburban areas are playing "catch-up" to land development. However, there is still opportunity to impress an open-space priority at all levels: regional, community, and project. Once established, various forms and scales of open space can help contain development or target it to desirable locations, promote ecologically sustainable regions, create connections between neighborhoods and between patches of open space, and provide a transition or buffer between different land areas.

Shaping growth. At a regional level, parks and open space greenbelts are tools that can help manage growth. These green necklaces define the limits of a community and discourage growth beyond those limits. Consider Boulder, Colorado, and Jacksonville, Florida. Boulder established an urban growth boundary in 1959 and shortly thereafter began purchasing open space to reinforce it. Forty years later, Jacksonville launched the Preservation Project. To date, the city has partnered with state and federal agencies to preserve more than 50,000 acres of land surrounding the city (Jacksonville n.d.).

Rather than purchase open space to create a growth boundary, some cities use open space to redirect growth. This technique is still in use. Like San Antonio, Austin also depends upon water from the Edwards Aquifer. Austin's strategy is to build new parks and provide desirable public services in "desired development zones," away from the aquifer's recharge zone, thereby encouraging more sustainable development.

At a local and project level, parks and open space can shape development by providing open space as an amenity around which to attract people. During the City Beautiful movement, planners employed the power of parks and boulevards to target residential development. In the late 1980's, Vancouver, British Columbia, began creating the North False Creek area, which provides an excellent example of using parks and open space to shape development. The waterfront site includes "central" parks, greenways, and open space buffers as a preliminary layer of urban design structure (City of Vancouver).

Bioregionalism. Preserving open space is a key tool in coordinating environmental sustainability with human settlement. This concept—bioregionalism—is both a philosophical and practical approach to planning that uses ecological systems as the organizing principal for land development. It requires that planners focus on the "unique biogeographical areas sharing cultural, economic and historical characteristics, distinguished by interdependent and interconnected ecological resources, which influence a region's economic development, cultural history, land use patterns, environmental quality, and ecological carrying capacity, and integrity. . . . [Bioregionalism] removes artificial boundaries that serve only human needs" (Callahan 1993). Examples of bioregions are watersheds, coastal areas, valleys, key habitats, and migration routes.

Bioregionalism, parks, and open space planning are connected on many levels and scales. For instance, preservation of open space and natural areas is critical to maintaining key habitat areas. This may require the protection of large tracts of land at a state or county level, as well as preservation of greenway connections at a local level. A watershed-based bioregional plan may recommend that all communities within the planning area, regardless of jurisdictional boundaries, require 150-foot buffers along a river and its tributaries. The buffer may be a function of a zoning ordinance, and it may also be a component of a greenway plan.

At a regional level, parks and open space greenbelts are tools that can help manage growth. These green necklaces define the limits of a community and discourage growth beyond those limits.

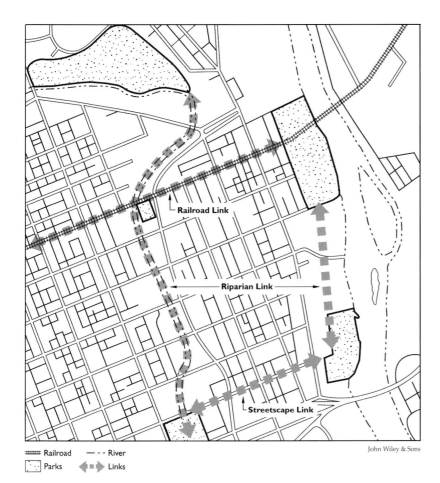

Railroad Link

Riparian Link

Streetscape Link

Railroad   — - - River
Parks   Links

John Wiley & Sons

In order to maximize the utility of parks, greenways, corridors, and trails, for example, connections need to be made between them. Planning a park and open space system should maximize the number of possible connections to truly create a "system."

Connections. One of the key components of urban form is connectivity, and it is most often considered in terms of streets. We can also create a different layer of connectivity in terms of parks and open space. Linear parks and greenways can connect parks to each other, forming a green network or pattern of open space. In typical parks and open space plans, these connections are usually along riparian or utility corridors. On occasion, the connections will be made via streetscapes. To be most effective, jurisdictions should design and preserve these connections prior to development, rather than trying to shoehorn in linkages afterwards.

Another form of connection can be found in design guidelines. While most park and open space plans do not specify them, design guidelines can be an effective way of unifying a park system. When tied to guidelines for neighborhoods and districts, park design guidelines can create cohesiveness throughout the entire form.

Buffers. Parks can also serve to disconnect. Parks and open space make good buffers between incompatible uses or can form physical barriers to noise, dust, and traffic. Parks can also serve as transition areas, providing spatial definition within developments or between neighborhoods. Fairbanks, Alaska, has even created a zoning definition for open space buffers. The Open Space Buffer (OSB) District was added to the zoning code in 2000 after the city recognized that none of the existing zones, including the Outdoor Recreation (OR) District, were appropriate for a true greenbelt/buffer area. The OR District allows vegetation to be cleared and intensive development of recreational facilities to occur—uses incompatible with a functional greenbelt/buffer. The OSB district is "intended to encourage open space and preserve natural vegetative buffers . . . and allow(s) minimal clearing of living vegetative growth only after a conditional use has been granted" (FNSBC 18.11.010). The only permitted use in the OSB district is maintenance of existing trails (Fairbanks County 2006).

CONCLUSION

As I hope I've made clear by now, parks are places; they are places that function on a number of levels to achieve a number of goals for a community. In order to create healthy, vital cities, parks and open spaces must be well-designed and woven into the urban fabric. Open space must be a priority in both systemwide and project-level planning. We must abandon the practice of relegating open space to unbuildable areas or leftover land. Parks and open space cannot be an afterthought. They are not a frill. They are essential.

What needs to happen is a raising of consciousness—and this PAS Report and all the output of APA's City Parks Forum hopes it has helped and will continue to help achieve this enlightenment—to make clear to citizens, municipal officials, park advocates, and planners the many diverse functions parks serve or can serve. The description I have provided above of the role of parks in creating communities of lasting value is comprehensive. But others may still find ways in which parks further contribute to creating community, promoting life, and responding to new issues (e.g., the role of parks in meeting the challenges of community health and global climate change are quite recent; others are certain to arise over time).

This is not wishful thinking. It is backed by research in numerous areas, making it clear that parks have champions in a number of disciplines and are more than worth the investment they require to ensure the creation and maintenance of healthy, sustainable, beautiful communities.

Danish architect Jan Gehl states that "the proper hierarchy of planning is life, space, and buildings, not buildings, space, and life" (Gehl 1987). While his quotation was in reference to the relationship between social value and the public realm, it can be a simple mantra to guide planning that effectively covers the life-enhancing properties—in the broadest sense of "life," both natural and social—of parks and open space.

The holistic benefits of parks call, in turn, for holistic planning. Systemwide considerations, in addition to site-specific responses, are necessary to do a good job of connecting all the various functions of parks to meeting the goals of a truly vibrant community. A confederation of interests can and should be put together to give parks the priority they deserve and the opportunity they present to create vibrant, sustainable communities.

CHAPTER 2 REFERENCES

American Forests. "Urban Ecosystem Analysis Atlanta Metro Area, Calculating the Value of Nature." August 2001. https://www.americanforests.org/downloads/rea/AF_Atlanta.pdf

Attorney General of California. "Proposition 84, Official Title and Summary." http://ss.ca.gov/elections/vig_06/general_06/pdf/proposition_84/entire_prop84.pdf

Beveridge, Charles, and C. Hoffman. eds. 1997. *The Papers of Frederick Law Olmsted: Supplementary Series Volume I, Writings on Parks, Parkways, and Park Systems*. Baltimore, Md.: Johns Hopkins University Press.

Bodin, Maria, and Terry Hartig. 2003. "Does the Outdoor Environment Matter for Psychological Restoration Gained through Running?" *Psychology of Sport and Exercise* 4, no. 2 (April).

Brownson, Ross C., Housemann, Robyn A., Brown, David R., Jackson-Thompson, Jeannette, King, Abby C., Malone, Bernard R., Sallis, James F. 2000. "Promoting Physical Activity in Rural Communities—Walking Trail Access, Use and Effects." *American Journal of Preventive Medicine* 18, no. 3 (April): 235–41

Callahan, Keane. 1993. "Bioregionalism: Wiser Planning for the Environment." *Land Use Law & Zoning Digest* 45, no. 8.

Chawla, Louise, and Debra Flanders Cushing. 2007. "Benefits of Nature for Children's Health." Design Fact Sheet #1. Denver: University of Colorado at Denver and Health Sciences Center, Children, Youth and Environments Center for Research.

"City Parks Forum Proceedings, Reno 2002." The City Parks Forum, American Planning Association. http://www.planning.org/cpf/pdf/charlotte.pdf

Cornfield, California, State Park Advisory Committee. 2003. *A Unified Vision for Cornfield State Park*. Sacramento: California State Parks. http://www.parks.ca.gov/pages/21299/files/recommendationsreport.pdf

Cortright, Joe. 2005. "The Young and Restless in a Knowledge Economy." *CEO's for Cities Report*, December 2005.

Coutts, John. ed. 2006. "Pennsylvania Organization for Watersheds and Rivers." *Watershed Weekly* 7, no. 44, November 3.

Crompton, John L. 2001. "The Impact of Parks on Property Values: a Review of the Empirical Evidence."" *Journal of Leisure Research* 33, no.1: 1–31.

———. 2002. *Parks and Economic Development*. Planning Advisory Service Report No. 502. Chicago: American Planning Association.

Dudley, Nigel, and Sue Stolton. 2003. "Running Pure: The Importance of Forest Protected Areas to Drinking Water." A World Bank/WWF Alliance for Forest Conservation and Sustainable Use Report. August.

Economic Research Associates. 2005. *Real Estate Impact Review of Parks and Recreation*. ERA Project No. 15543. March. http://www.ilparks.org/research_era_real_estate.pdf

Fairbanks, Alaska, County of. 2006. *County Department of Community Planning Staff Report, RZ2007-005*. http://www.co.fairbanks.ak.us/meetings/Planning Commission/2006meetings/080106/RZ2007-005.pdf

Frumkin, Howard. 2003. "Healthy Places: Exploring the Evidence." *American Journal of Public Health* 93, no. 9 (September).

Gehl, Jan. 1987. *The Space Between Buildings*. New York: Van Nostrand Reinhold.

Girling, Cynthia. 2005. "Green Infrastructure: A Future for Urban Landscapes." *Sitelines Annual* (January): 19–21.

Grahn, P. 1990. In *Parks for the Future*, edited by G.J. Sorte. Alnarp, Sweden: Movium.

Jacksonville, Florida, City of. n.d. Parks and Recreation Website. http://www.coj.net/Departments/Parks+and+Recreation/Preservation+Project/

Kaplan, R., and S. Kaplan. 1998. *With People in Mind: Design and Management for Everyday Nature*. Washington, D.C.: Island Press.

Kuo, Francis E., William C. Sullivan, C. Coley, and L. Brunson. 1998. "Fertile Ground for Community: Inner-city Neighborhood Common Spaces." *American Journal of Community Psychology* 26, no. 6: 823–51.

Lieberman, Gerald A., and Linda L. Hoody. 1998. *Closing the Achievement Gap: Using the Environment as an Integral Context for Learning*. San Diego, Calif.: State Education and Environment Roundtable. http://www.seer.org/extras/execsum.pdf

Massachusetts Bay Transportation Authority. 1982. *Southwest Corridor Project Booklet*. October. http://www.mbta.com/

Ministry of the Environment, Government of Japan. 2004. *Outline of the Policy Framework to Reduce Urban Heat Island Effects*. March. http://www.env.go.jp/en/air/heat/heatisland.pdf

Moore, Robin. 2003. "How Cities Use Parks to Help Children Learn." City Parks Forum Briefing Paper. Chicago: American Planning Association.

Nicholls, Sarah. 2004. "Measuring the Impact of Parks on Property Values." *Parks and Recreation* 39, no. 3 (March): 24–36.

Oldenburg, Ray. 1996. "Our Vanishing Third Places." *Planning Commissioner's Journal* 25 (Winter): 10.

Perlman, Dan L., and Jeffrey C. Milder. 2005. *Practical Ecology For Planners, Developers, and Citizens*. Washington, D.C.: Island Press.

Shore, Debra. 1997. "Editor's Note." *Chicago Wilderness* (Fall): 3.

Spronken-Smith, R.A., and T.R. Oke. 1999. "Scale Modeling of Nocturnal Cooling in Urban Parks." *Boundary-Layer Meteorology* 93, no. 2 (November): 287–312

Stout, Heidi. 2001. "Pioneer Courthouse Square 's Nordstrom Building Changes Hands." *Portland Business Journal*, August 29, 2001

Trust for Public Land. n.d. Website. http://www.tpl.org/tier3_cd.cfm?content_item_id=19939&folder_id=905

Turner, Tom. 1996. *City as Landscape: A Post-Postmodern View of Planning and Design*. http://www.gardenvisit.com/landscape/architecture/16.1-park-character.htm

Uhlir, Edward. 2006. "The Millennium Park Effect." *Pennsylvania Economy League Report* (Winter): 20–26.

Ulrich, Roger S. 1984. "View Through a Window May Influence Recovery from Surgery." *Science* 224, April 27, pp. 420–21.

Urban Forest Ecosystems Institute, Trees for the Millennium. n.d. Website. http://www.ufei.org/trees.html

Vancouver, British Columbia, City of. 2006. *False Creek Plan*. http://www.city.vancouver.bc.ca/commsvcs/currentplanning/urbandesign/br2pdf/falsecreek.pdf

Wilson, Edward O. 1984. *Biophilia*. Cambridge, Mass.: Harvard University Press.

Wolf, Kathleen L. 1998. *Urban Forest Values: Economic Benefit of Trees in Cities*. Seattle: Center for Urban Horticulture, University of Washington, November.

CHAPTER 3

How Do You Effectively Assess a Community's Need for Parks and Open Space?

By David Barth, AICP

As described in Chapters 1 and 2, the definitions and functions of parks and park systems have changed significantly over the past 150 years. Communities and lifestyles have become more diverse and complex, and parks and open space needs now vary widely among individuals, families, and neighborhoods. So, given these new definitions and functions, the variety of constituencies that park agencies must serve, and the potential role for new partners (e.g., health agencies), how does one conduct a needs assessment that goes beyond the typical fixation with a demographic standard (i.e., X acres of parks and open space per each 1,000 in population)? This chapter hopes to provide some guidance. You will also find an actual needs assessment done for Oviedo, Florida, in Appendix A of this PAS Report.

There is no standard method or single, authoritative source regarding how to properly conduct a parks, recreation, and open space needs assessment. Planners, urban designers, park designers and other planning professionals most commonly use the findings from a parks, recreation, and open space needs assessment to determine:

- residents' level of satisfaction with existing facilities, programs, and services;

- community needs, priorities, and preferences for various types of parks, facilities and/or programs; and

- residents' willingness and/or preferences to fund needed improvements, facilities, and programs.

Using this data, decision makers can be more specific about the changes needed in policies, programs, staffing, and funding. Another purpose for a needs assessment is to engage the public in a dialogue regarding the community's values, quality-of-life criteria, and long-range vision. While a needs assessment is essentially a "gap analysis," identifying and measuring the gaps between existing and ideal conditions, "ideal conditions" vary among communities, and the needs assessment process provides the opportunity to define them according to a community's specific values and interests.

David Barth

Parks and recreation needs have become much more diverse.

TRIANGULATION AND ASSESSMENT TOOLS

When selecting the most appropriate technique for an effective needs assessment, a particularly useful concept is "triangulation"; that is, considering need from at least three vantage points. Triangulation helps to differentiate between community *needs* (of which there are often many) and community *priorities* (the greatest common needs of the community). An assessment conducted solely from the vantage point of organized sports leagues, for example, may indicate that additional sports fields are the greatest need in a community. Yet the reality may be (and often is) that safe bikeways and quiet sitting areas are more important to most residents than sports fields. The practice of triangulation helps ensure a more accurate assessment of community priorities.

The three types of assessment tools typically used in triangulation include anecdotal, qualitative, and quantitative techniques.

Anecdotal techniques, while sometimes the most valid assessment tools, are probably the least scientific. Examples of anecdotal techniques include site visits and photographs, telephone or face-to-face conversations with facility or program participants, personal observations, discussions with parks and recreation staff, and other types of similar discussions and observations.

Outputs from these activities, if properly recorded and documented, can form the initial components of a needs assessment.

Qualitative techniques involve talking with a wide cross-section of community residents and stakeholders to identify common themes, needs, and interests. While not as scientific and objective as quantitative techniques (see below), qualitative techniques can provide insights into community issues, "hidden agendas," and emotions. Planners should first identify the community leaders, activists, and providers to include in the process, and then select the appropriate technique(s) for each. One parks planner, for example, advocates identifying "the top 100 community leaders" to interview. Alternative qualitative forums and techniques include the following:

- Staff interviews and workshops
- Interviews with elected officials and community leaders
- Interviews with representatives of public school boards, nonprofit organizations, and other parks and recreation providers
- Focus group meetings with teens, adults, seniors, youth and adult sports leagues, cultural groups, environmental organizations, and other special interest groups
- Workshops with elected officials, staff, advisory groups, neighborhood residents, steering committees, and other community representatives.

Quantitative techniques often have the greatest credibility because most people have faith in numbers and formulas. Numbers can be manipulated, however, to support various positions, so quantitative techniques should never be used alone to determine community needs and priorities. Typical quantitative techniques include measuring park acreage, counting the number of recreation facilities, and defining geographic service areas based on national, state, or local guidelines. Examples include the following:

- Acreage level of service (number of acres per 1,000 population)
- Facilities level of service (number of facilities per 1,000 population)
- Park and recreation facility service areas (e.g., a neighborhood park may serve every residence within a half-mile radius)

Bike trails and paths are a top priority in many communities. Here is a "Rails-to-Trails" conversion.

Glatting Jackson Kercher Anglin

Other quantitative techniques that can be used to add to these findings include the following:

- Comparing a community's resources, such as acreage, facilities, staff, and budget, against those of other communities of a similar size and demographic composition
- Measuring existing capacity versus demand for various facilities and programs
- Measuring per capita investment in parks (replacement value of land and facilities) by planning or political district
- Conducting a telephone, mail, or web survey regarding needs and priorities

A valid needs assessment process does not need to include all of these techniques, but at least two techniques should be used from each of the three categories. The two most important anecdotal techniques are site visits to observe existing conditions and recording staff insights from interactions with the community. These will provide a basic "feel" for the community's most pressing needs.

The two most effective qualitative techniques are interviews with elected officials and a workshop with a project steering committee or advisory committee comprised of a broad cross-section of community leaders, recreation providers, and residents. Elected officials often have real insights into the needs of their constituents, and the interviews also provide a chance to learn about what parks or recreation improvements are most important to each official. The steering committee workshop provides an opportunity for candid and informed discussions regarding community needs and priorities.

The two most important quantitative techniques are a statistically valid survey and a geographic service area analysis based on local values. The survey is the only tool that can accurately poll community residents regarding their priorities and preferences. And the service area analysis reveals voids in equitable access to parks and recreation facilities throughout the community.

When designing a needs assessment process, planners must first clarify their objectives and begin with the end result in mind.

DESIGNING A NEEDS ASSESSMENT PROCESS

When designing a needs assessment process, planners must first clarify their objectives and begin with the end result in mind. Key questions to answer when designing a process include:

- What do I want to find out that I don't already know? Am I testing a specific hypothesis (e.g., we may need more neighborhood parks)? Do I want to find out how residents feel about parks in general? Do I want resident input regarding specific issues, such as the acquisition or development of a specific park site?
- What is the scope of my assessment? Should the needs assessment focus only on parks, or should it also include other elements of a comprehensive parks system (as discussed in Chapters 1 and 2), such as recreation facilities, environmental lands, trails, streetscapes, and cultural sites? For example, many needs assessments reveal that the top parks and recreation needs in a community are "shaded sidewalks and bike lanes," which are part of the larger parks system concept. This need may not be addressed if the question is not asked in the needs assessment.
- Do I want residents' feedback regarding the need for specific types of parks, specific recreation or leisure interests, or specific park characteristics? Chapter 2 discusses various park attributes (e.g., opportunities for contemplation, spontaneity), characteristics (e.g., accessibility, beauty), and activities (e.g., walking, swimming, picnicking). Needs assessment

techniques and questions will vary depending upon the type of feedback desired. For example, a public workshop where residents create collages of words and photographs describing desired character may help to determine community preferences for park characteristics.

- Who am I trying to reach? Do I want to differentiate the needs and desires of specific geographic areas? If that is the case, different techniques are required to gather information from individual neighborhoods and wards, for example, than from ones that would be used for a broader citywide or countywide assessment.

- Who are the key stakeholders to involve? Develop a method to identify the stakeholders for a planning process. In addition to involving elected officials, recreation providers, staff, and residents, for instance, one might want to identify community leaders with influence and "ability to reason."

Glatting Jackson Kercher Anglin

Collages can be used to describe desired park characteristics.

- What data are available? If I believe that private or nonprofit parks and recreation facilities (e.g., YMCAs, planned unit development amenity areas, and churches) can help meet residents' needs for parks, do I have an accurate map and inventory showing acreage and numbers of facilities? Do I have accurate maps and inventory data regarding other types of parks, trails, natural areas, sports fields, and other park types of facilities (based on the scope of the needs assessment)? And are the data in a usable mapping format (e.g., AutoCAD or GIS)?

- What demographic and population data are available? Do we have accurate information regarding residents' ages, ethnicities, and income levels? Do we understand the differences in demographics among neighborhoods? Are the data available in a GIS format for analysis?

- Are there specific issues to research? Many needs assessments ask specific questions about funding, such as residents' willingness to support bond issues, sales tax increases, or user fee increases. Needs assessments are also sometimes used to seek residents' feedback about the acquisition or development of a specific park site or to ask about other specific community issues.

- How will the information be used? Will the needs assessment be used as the basis for a parks and open space master plan, an update of the community's comprehensive plan, or a bond referendum? The way planners will use information has a direct relationship to the types of specific questions and techniques they should employ.
- Who will review and approve the findings? A needs assessment process is practically useless if no one agrees with the findings! A typical review and approval process includes the involvement of agency staff, a project steering/advisory committee (oftentimes comprised of the community's parks and recreation advisory board, plus other key stakeholders), elected officials, and the general public. Each group needs to participate in the process and approve the findings. If consensus regarding the findings is not reached, additional needs assessment techniques may be required; for example, if the findings from an initial survey and other needs assessment techniques prove inconclusive, additional surveys or workshops may be required.

In addition, planners must also ask how they will manage the needs assessment process. Typical project management questions include:

- Do we have the internal expertise to conduct the process, or would we benefit from outside expertise? Some agencies feel that to avoid any perception of agency bias, it is important to hire an outside consultant who will serve as a neutral facilitator in the process and provide insights based on experience with similar projects.
- What is our budget? Many agencies contact consultants or other agencies to determine the scope and costs of similar projects in order to establish a budget.
- What is our schedule? A typical needs assessment process, using an outside consultant, takes three to six months. In some cases, a critical issue (e.g., preparation in advance of a bond referendum or an election) may drive the schedule, so planners need to determine if specific deadlines must be met.

If this design leads to information substantive enough to make decisions and if stakeholders and decision makers consider that information accurate and legitimate, the design has been successful.

THE NEEDS ASSESSMENT PROCESS

A parks and open space needs assessment has three specific steps: 1) analyze existing conditions; 2) decide which techniques to use; and 3) build consensus around the findings.

Analyze Existing Conditions

Every needs assessment relies on a thorough understanding of the current system. How can you tell what you need if you don't know what you have? The components of the existing conditions study include an accurate base map and inventories of parklands, facilities, programs, and users. Many agencies, unfortunately, do not maintain up-to-date records of park types and acreage, numbers of facilities, park conditions, park attendance, and other similar data. Consequently, the task of mapping, inventorying, and analyzing existing conditions is often a more difficult and time-consuming task than anticipated.

Here I describe four components of the existing conditions analysis: data collection, base map preparation, analysis of demographics and lifestyles, and park site visits.

Every needs assessment relies on a thorough understanding of the current system. How can you tell what you need if you don't know what you have?

Data collection. The first task in assessing existing conditions is to collect and update available data. The data you will need to do an effective analysis of existing conditions include:

- the comprehensive plan;
- the current and future land-use maps;

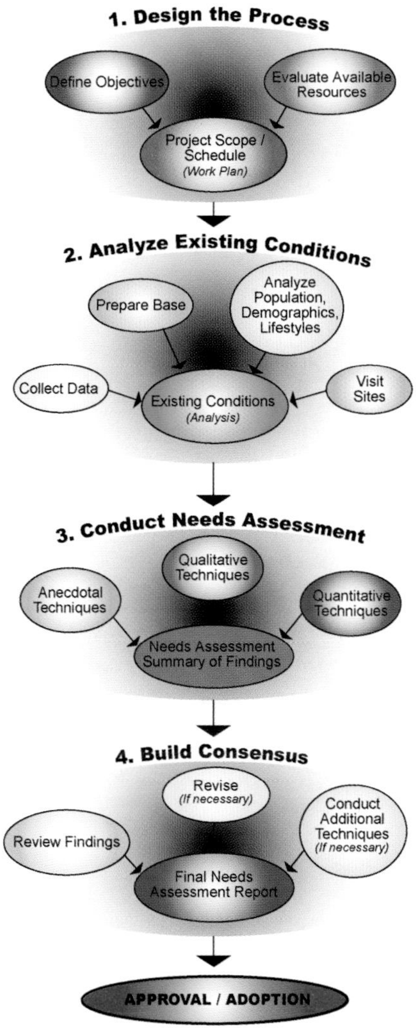

FIGURE 3-1. NEEDS ASSESSMENT PROCESS DIAGRAM

Source: Glatting Jackson Kercher Anglin

- current maps and inventories (acreage and facilities) of all public parks and recreation facilities and trails and bikeways within three to five miles of the jurisdiction;
- a current inventory of school, church, and nonprofit facilities and services;
- a current inventory of private recreation facilities;
- the capital improvements program (CIP), and the community's fix-and-replacement budget (FARB);
- population and demographics data, both current and projected;
- recreation program brochures, catalogs, and flyers;

- a list of current sports leagues (youth and adult), program levels, and schedules; and

- aerial photographs of the community.

Once the data are collected, they must be checked for accuracy. It is terribly frustrating (and potentially embarrassing) to find out midway through a needs assessment process that data are inaccurate or obsolete, and assumptions based on the data are wrong. Once the data are confirmed, date and file them for easy reference; the needs assessment process may take from three to six months to complete, so the data must remain accessible for review or updating.

Base map preparation. A base map of the existing parks and recreation system should be developed in AutoCAD or a GIS, showing actual boundaries of all public parks and recreation facilities, as well as:

- current and future land uses;

- existing and proposed roadways;

- public (city, county, and state) parks and recreation facilities;

- trails, sidewalks, and bikeways;

- school sites;

- church sites;

- the sites on nonprofit groups who may have recreation programs and services;

- the public parks and recreation facilities in adjacent communities;

- existing private or nonprofit recreation and cultural facilities;

- vacant and derelict lands;

- major power line utility easements and other "gray infrastructure";

- natural and man-made features (e.g., lakes, canals, wetlands, and floodplains);

- natural open space and conservation areas;

- threatened or endangered species habitat; and

- natural hazard areas.

To get an accurate understanding of the existing system, extend the base map three to five miles beyond the boundaries of the jurisdiction conducting the needs assessment. Most residents do not differentiate between city and county parks, for example, and often they use the facility closest to home regardless of ownership or jurisdiction.

GIS is a powerful data management tool and should be used if the needs assessment will include service area analyses, demographic analyses, or other complex mapping and data analysis techniques. It is a complex mapping tool, however, and it should not be used if the only purpose is to develop a base map; when that product is desired, AutoCAD is a preferable mapping tool.

The analysis of demographics and lifestyles. The existing conditions analysis must also include an evaluation of current and anticipated users. GIS mapping can be used to identify demographic trends and patterns in a community, including demographic differences among neighborhoods. Differences in demographics may translate into differences in parks and recreation needs. For example, Ho (2005, 281) points out a "significant variation" in the parks and recreation preferences and perceptions of different ethnic groups. One study Ho cites indicates that "Hispanics and Asians had significantly higher participation in picnicking than Blacks," for example, while another study showed that "minority group members were more

GIS is a powerful data management tool and should be used if the needs assessment will include service area analyses, demographic analyses, or other complex mapping and data analysis techniques.

likely to engage in passive social-oriented activities (e.g., picnicking and socializing) while Whites were involved most in active individual sorts such as walking and jogging" (Ho 2005, 286). There are obvious dangers in making such generalities—always validate this type of academic information through neighborhood workshops, interviews, and other needs assessment techniques.

It may also be useful to translate demographic data into lifestyle profiles. Market research companies, such as ESRI and Civitas, provide "lifestyle" or "psychographic" research that provides profiles of various market segments (e.g., "Upscale Avenues," "Solo Acts," "Senior Styles," "Laptops and Lattes," and "Family Portrait"). Each profile includes attributes and preferences of the market segment, including recreation preferences. According to Vorhees (2006), the recreation preferences of the "Solo Act" segment (young, single, highly educated city dwellers) include tennis, volleyball, baseball, golf, ice skating, snorkeling, and yoga. A lifestyle analysis of a community's population could be a useful component of an existing conditions analysis.

Park site visits. Site visits are a critical component of the existing conditions analysis. In addition to providing an opportunity to observe conditions first hand, site visits also provide opportunities for informal interviews with park users and staff. Document site visits in both text and photographs. Typical categories of analysis include:

- existing park conditions, including the condition and appearance of existing facilities and amenities, and the need for improved maintenance, repairs, or replacements;

- park accessibility, including vehicular, bicycle, pedestrian, and ADA access both into and within the park;

- park functionality, including the ability to accommodate both organized and nonorganized activities, and the park's ability to perform its intended function (e.g., neighborhood park, community park, sports complex); and

- park context, including compatibility and conflicts (e.g., noise, lights, traffic, and parking) with adjacent land uses.

Techniques that Make for an Effective Needs Assessment

Once planners have documented the existing system and analyzed that data, they need to choose which needs assessment techniques they will use. As discussed above, the three most typical tools rely on anecdotal, qualitative, and quantitative techniques. A robust needs assessment process uses at least two or three techniques from each category to "triangulate" the results.

Anecdotal techniques. Anecdotal techniques often provide the first impressions of community needs. The analysis of the existing system, casual conversations with park users and program participants, and conversations with park, facility, and program staff often provide great insights into community issues and priorities. If parks are poorly maintained and used, for example, the top priority may be for park renovation or an increased maintenance budget prior to acquiring additional parkland for new facilities. On the other hand, anecdotal data (e.g., "we've had to turn away hundreds of kids from Little League because there just aren't enough fields") could be the first indication that more parkland is needed.

A cautionary note—anecdotal techniques can be very misleading! For example, one reason a community may "turn away hundreds of kids" is because they come from another jurisdiction, and the community has made a policy decision to serve only community residents. So, while anecdotal evidence can provide a first impression, it needs to be verified through quantitative

Glatting Jackson Kercher Anglin

Casual interviews with park users often provide first impressions of community needs.

Source: Glatting Jackson Kercher Anglin

Steering committees or advisory committee workshops are an important component of successful needs assessment processes. Here a committee works in Miami-Dade County.

and qualitative techniques, and it should certainly never be used as the sole basis of determining needs.

Qualitative techniques. Qualitative techniques involve interviews, meetings, and workshops with a wide cross-section of community representatives who may have their "fingers on the pulse" of the community. Qualitative techniques usually include two components: 1) an educational or informational presentation providing an overview of park systems generally, the purpose of a needs assessment, and a review of the community's existing system; and 2) interviews with or surveys of participants regarding needs and priorities. A simple, standard questionnaire should be developed so that responses can be easily compared and tabulated; a shortened version of the mail or telephone survey is often useful. Typical interview questions include:

- What do you believe are the greatest community needs for parks, open space, or recreation? Provide respondents with a list of park system components, defined by the scope of the needs assessment.

- If additional parkland or facilities are needed, which funding techniques would you support? Provide respondents with a list of potential funding sources.

- What partnerships would you support? Provide examples of partnerships.

Of all of the qualitative techniques, interviews with elected officials and other community leaders are one of the most important. These are the people who will ultimately be responsible for supporting or approving the findings from the needs assessment, and recommending funding, policies, and programs. It is critical to engage them early in the process and to keep them informed. They are also some of the best-informed participants, and their opinions are usually consistent with findings from the other needs assessment techniques.

An equally important qualitative technique is the steering committee or advisory committee workshop, especially given the chance for new partnerships to support park planning and funding, as noted in Chapter 2. Choose committee members with care. They should represent a cross-section of the community, including community leaders, parks and recreation providers, potential partners (schools, churches, and other jurisdictions, for example), teenagers, seniors, business and tourism officials, and others. Some communities begin with their existing parks and recreation boards or committees and add new members to create a 20- to 30-person committee. Similar to the elected officials, committee members are often some of the best-informed and most influential members of the community, and their input and support of the process is critical.

These workshops can function in several ways. During the needs assessment planning process, the committee can be asked to review and comment on the process method, including making recommendations for the specific needs assessment techniques that the committee feels will be most effective and beneficial to the community. During the needs assessment itself, it can complete survey questionnaires and provide information regarding the opinions of committee members about community needs and priorities. And during the final consensus-building phase of the process (discussed in more detail below), they can review and comment on the findings before they are presented to the elected officials.

Focus group meetings with teens, adults, seniors, youth and adult sports leagues, environmental and cultural organizations, and other special interest groups are another common qualitative technique. These meetings are useful to understand specific community needs. The same interview questionnaire given to the committee members can be used, and groups should be encouraged to speak freely about their needs.

Note that a "need" may not be a "priority." For example the need for a new competition swimming pool may be important to an aquatics focus group, but it may be a low priority for the population in general. Again, triangulation is valuable because it compares the needs from one technique to another to determine common community needs and priorities.

The most common qualitative technique, the public workshop, is often the least useful. Public workshops must be well advertised and attended to represent a true cross-section of the community. Unfortunately, this is not usually the case. Ideas to increase attendance include:

Glatting Jackson Kercher Anglin

Martin County Parks & Recreation Department

Focus group meetings are a useful technique to determine the needs of special interest groups, like these young people (left) in Palm City, Florida. The notice from Martin County (above) breaks out various user groups' interests for meetings.

- conduct kick-off events and promotions to let people know about the needs assessment process;
- schedule meetings at multiple locations throughout the community, preferably in each neighborhood;
- conduct meetings on Saturday mornings or other convenient times; and
- offer food or entertainment to encourage people to participate.

The format for public workshops usually involves some type of short introductory presentation to familiarize participants with the purpose and methodology of the needs assessment process, asking participants to fill out survey questionnaires, and sometimes conducting an informal poll to determine the top priorities of the people in attendance. If multiple workshops are conducted, the findings from each workshop should be summarized individually in order to track geographic differences in needs.

Visioning processes provide an opportunity to identify needs by developing a long-range vision of what a community would like to become, and comparing the vision to the existing condition, to identify voids or gaps. The vision is based on community values or quality-of-life criteria, developed

The Miami-Dade County Visioning Workshop provided an opportunity to brainstorm community needs based on the development of a long-range vision.

by a community's staff, advisory committee, residents, and elected officials. For example, in my firm's work, we begin a visioning process with a review of the following framework for an ideal park system:

- Central gathering spaces and civic buildings for public events
- Small parks, playgrounds, or squares within one-quarter mile of every resident
- Walk-to parks, easily accessible to every resident
- Community centers and parks easily accessible to every resident
- Approximately 50 percent of park space preserved in natural or maintained open space
- Equitably distributed system of sports complexes and other special use facilities

The community needs developed in the visioning process, shown in the photo on the opposite page, resulted in a detailed map illustrating the potential parks system for Miami-Dade County.

Glatting Jackson Kercher Anglin

- Co-location and joint use of schools, libraries, and parks
- Public access provided to beaches, rivers, lakes, and streams
- Natural areas protected as conservation lands, with appropriate and equitable public access
- An interconnected network of boulevards, parkways, streets, greenways, and trails designed as a communitywide system of linear parks, and pedestrian, bicycle, and transit access to every public park and open space
- Public art and signage integrated throughout the system to create sense of place
- Protection and celebration of significant cultural and historical sites
- Equitable access to social, recreation, and wellness programs
- Parks planned as catalysts for neighborhood stabilization or redevelopment
- Parks designed to create opportunities for Transit-Oriented Development (TOD)
- Greenbelts surrounding urban development areas to contain sprawl or buffer agricultural or environmental lands
- Parks designed to reduce energy and water consumption, to serve as models for sustainable development
- Neighborhood and community-level public involvement
- Well designed and maintained facilities
- Municipal, county, state, federal, corporate, and nonprofit partnerships
- Civic leaders and champions
- Community-building mindset

Every needs assessment process should include at least two or three quantitative assessment techniques.

These criteria are modified based on a community's values, and a vision plan is created to reflect the application of the criteria to existing conditions. Identifying the gaps between existing and ideal conditions is an effective technique for identifying long-range needs.

Quantitative techniques. Every needs assessment process should include at least two or three quantitative assessment techniques. Elected officials and other decision makers want to see some type of quantitative analysis that validates the findings from the other techniques. Quantitative techniques can also yield some surprising trends or patterns, especially if conducted repeatedly over a period of years. For example, since 1968, Miami-Dade County, Florida, has been conducting Leisure Interest Surveys every three to four years, and that data provide interesting insights into changing demographics and parks and recreation needs.

A common quantitative technique that generates a great deal of discussion and debate is establishing a Level of Service (LOS) for parks and recreation facilities. Public agencies have historically used LOS to establish and measure the adequacy of most basic public services. Services, such as police, fire, roadways, sewer and water supply, can all be measured quantitatively using an established LOS.

No universally accepted LOS standards for parks and recreation facilities exist, but many federal, state, and local agencies have established guidelines. Florida's *State Comprehensive Outdoor Recreation Plan* (SCORP), for example, recommends a minimum LOS of two acres per 1,000 population for neighborhood parks; two acres per 1,000 population for community parks; and four acres per 1,000 for regional parks. While it is sometimes tempting to save both time and money by relying on state or federal standards or guidelines to determine community needs, it is unrealistic to expect that these standards will apply equally to communities with different climates, cultures, and demographics. Florida's SCORP, for example, makes the disclaimer that "these guidelines are intended for broad, statewide application, and make no allowances for localized differences in communities or in specific outdoor recreation environments. . . . Local jurisdictions particularly are encouraged to develop their own guidelines to more adequately reflect local conditions in determining recreation needs" (Spencer 2002, 4-1).

Similarly, the National Recreation and Park Association's *Park, Recreation, Open Space and Greenway Guidelines* provides a framework for park system planning, and an approach to developing a LOS standard for local communities but advises that "no single type of resource and facility guideline can adequately meet all outdoor recreation planning needs simultaneously. Each outdoor recreation provider should, therefore, select the guidelines that best serve its specific planning needs" (Mertes and Hall 1996, 61).

Planners interested in calculating specific LOS standards for their communities may wish to consider one or more of these three techniques: benchmarking, calculating facility LOS, and service area analysis.

1. *Benchmarking.* Many communities benchmark themselves to other similar communities by calculating and comparing:

- acres of park land per capita;
- parks and recreation spending per capita;
- maintenance budget per acre of park land or per capita;
- number of park staff per acre of park land; and
- appraised value of public investment in park land and facilities per capita

Data collected from comparable communities are often summarized in chart form to illustrate the LOS differences among communities. Obviously, if a community has much lower levels of park acreage, facilities, staff, or spending than other similar communities, this *may* be an indication that more is needed. As with all other needs assessment techniques, it may be necessary to validate the benchmarking by conducting additional research or comparing the findings to the results of other needs assessment techniques.

2. *Calculating facility LOS.* The NRPA Guidelines include a summary of Miami-Dade County's method for calculating its own LOS for individual recreation facilities, based on estimates of local supply and demand. The eight basic steps of this "demand analysis" include determining:

- park classifications;
- recreation activity menus;
- open space standards;
- present supply;
- expressed demand;
- minimum population service requirements;
- individual LOS for each park class; and
- total LOS for the entire park system

The NRPA *Guidelines* include a case study and formulas that planners can follow to complete their calculations.

3. *Service area analysis.* Many communities are placing more emphasis on equitable access to parks and recreation facilities than on the quantity of parklands or facilities. A service area analysis shows the geographic areas served by parks and recreation facilities based on community values. St. Petersburg, Florida, for example, has established a goal to build a playground within a half-mile of every resident. Denver has established a goal of a green space within six blocks of every resident (Harnik 2003). Once a community's

Planners interested in calculating specific LOS standards for their communities may wish to consider one or more of these three techniques: benchmarking, calculating facility LOS, and service area analysis.

goals or values have been established, a service area analysis can identify deficiencies in the system.

GreenPlay, LLC, a consulting firm in Broomfield, Colorado, has established an improved method for conducting a service area analysis. Their GRASP(c) Methodology (Geo-Referenced Amenities Standards Program) measures the service area that an individual community facility covers, such as a dog park or a playground. The amount of service delivered by various facilities can be calculated and displayed graphically to quickly identify gaps in service on a neighborhood, community, or regional basis. GRASP(c) also allows population density factors to be combined into traditional LOS equations. The GRASP(c) approach can be incorporated into mapping and tabular information that then can be used as management tools. The method provides information that helps guide decision makers and is also easily understood by the general public.

GreenPlay's GRASP© methodology analyzes level of service provided by specific facilities based on community values. Here is the chart for Brookline, Massachusetts.

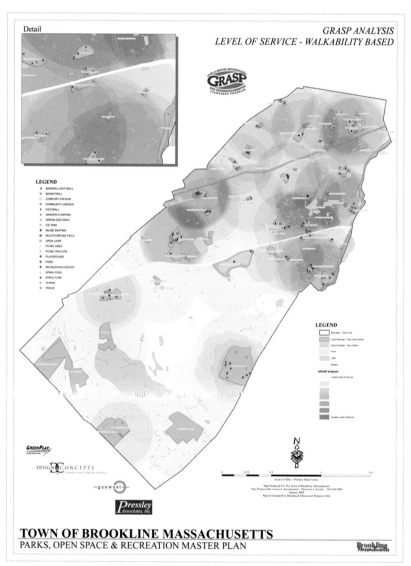

GreenPlay LLC

Of all of the quantitative techniques, random surveys are the most accurate and reliable. If conducted correctly, using a qualified statistician or professional researcher who can determine the appropriate sample size and design the most effective survey tool, a survey can yield results that most closely

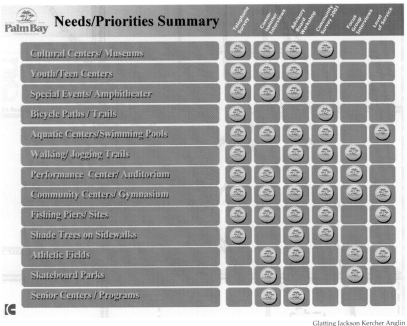

Glatting Jackson Kercher Anglin

A Needs Assessment Summary Chart should illustrate the answer to the question, Does my community need more parks?

reflect the opinions and feelings of community residents. Telephone, mail, and web-based surveys can all be effective needs assessment tools.

According to Robert Hays of Haysmar Incorporated, a behavioral research firm in Jupiter, Florida, benefits of a telephone survey include:

- assurance of even coverage by geographic area or other selected demographic identifier;
- assurance that the person being interviewed meets the necessary respondent qualifications;
- faster completion than other feasible methods;
- data immediately usable following the completion of the interview; and
- protection against manipulation of the results by special interest groups.

Leisure Vision/ETC Institute's IS Matrix allows residents and decision makers to discern top priority needs.

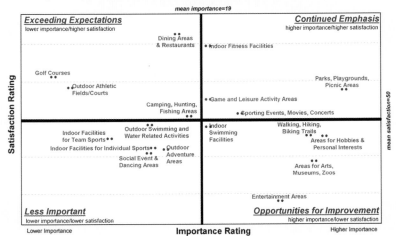

Source: *Leisure Vision/ETC Institute*

Leisure Vision/ETC Institute

Telephone surveys should be between five and seven minutes long, with questions either carefully focused on actionable issues or designed to provide answers to assist in making decisions. Depending on the types of questions used, five to seven minutes allows an interviewer to ask between 10 and 25 questions. Objective, short-answer questions allow a greater breadth of issues to be covered in the suggested time frame.

If the questions are properly formatted, the results can be cross-tabulated by age group, ethnicity, geographic location, or other demographic categories to provide more specific data. Telephone survey results can also be tabulated by ZIP code, or a mail survey can be used to supplement the findings and differentiate needs by location. Leisure Vision of Olathe, Kansas, a market research firm specializing in parks and recreation market research, uses a combination of mail and telephone surveys to get the best results.

BUILDING CONSENSUS REGARDING FINDINGS

Once the needs assessment techniques have been completed, document the findings to identify common themes, issues, and priorities. Top needs and priorities tend to "bubble up" in the process; that is, they consistently appear as a top priority regardless of the technique used. Planners may wish to "weight" some techniques more than others: for example, a 300-person telephone survey may have more weight than a public workshop attended by only three residents. The needs assessment summary chart shows one technique used to plot the results of various needs assessment techniques.

Leisure Vision uses another technique called an Importance/Satisfaction (I/S) Matrix to illustrate the results of their telephone surveys. The I/S matrix indicates that while some needs may be ranked "important" to a community, the need may also be "satisfied." For example, a community may feel that swimming pools are very important, but the need for swimming pools is being well met. Similarly, a community may decide that tennis courts are "not important," but that the need is not being met. Thus the top priority needs are those ranked both "important" and "not satisfied."

The results of the needs assessment findings should be presented to several groups, including staff, the steering committee or advisory committee, the public, and elected officials to build consensus regarding interpretation of the findings, and to discuss preliminary recommendations and actions. If consensus cannot be reached, additional needs assessment techniques (primarily quantitative) may be necessary. The needs assessment process can be considered successful only when there's broad-based acceptance of the findings and support for the proposed resultant actions. The findings can then be used to help develop a parks and open space system plan, as discussed in the next chapter.

CHAPTER 3 REFERENCES

Harnik, Peter. 2003. *The Excellent City Park System*. Washington, D.C.: The Trust for Public Land.

Ho, Ching-Hua, Vinod Sasidharan, and William Elmendorf. 2005. "Gender and Ethnic Variations in Urban Park Preferences, Visitation and Perceived Benefits." *Journal of Leisure Research*, Volume 37, Number 3. Ashburn, Va.: National Recreation and Park Association.

Mertes, James D. and James R. Hall. 1996. *Park, Recreation, Open Space and Greenway Guidelines*. Arlington, Va.: National Recreation and Park Association.

Reviere, R., S. Berkowitz, C. Carter, and C. Ferguson. 1996. *Needs Assessment: A Creative and Practical Guide for Social Scientists*. Washington, D.C.: Taylor & Francis.

Spencer, W. February 2002. *Outdoor Recreation in Florida—2000: Florida's Statewide Comprehensive Outdoor Recreation Plan*. Tallahassee, Fla.: Florida Department of Environmental Protection.

Voorhees, Rick. October 2006. "Understanding Cañada's Lifestyle and Psychographic Research." http://www.canadacollege.edu/inside/strategicplanning/docs/understanding-psychographic-research.pdf.

CHAPTER 4

Parks and Open Space System Plans

By Megan Lewis, AICP

While an element in a comprehensive plan can address a community's broad policies for parks and open space, it is the specific park plan that will implement the goals and vision expressed in the comprehensive plan element. To understand if the current state of the art of parks and open space planning was indeed meeting the broader principles and approaches discussed by the other authors of this report, I conducted an analysis of recently completed parks and open space plans, reviewing and comparing them according to 26 factors.

This chapter does not discuss each plan's planning process in detail. While there are commonalities among the plans, which are described further, this section focuses mainly on outstanding examples from the field. Because, as the authors of other chapters in this PAS Report have made clear, no plan can be a model for all communities, my goal is to showcase best practices and to identify key principles for park and open space planning.

THE CURRENT STATE OF THE ART IN PARK PLANS

To find examples of some of the best park planning practices currently underway, I generated a list of cities or city/county entities known for their park systems, surveyed the plans of participants in the City Parks Forum program, and considered plans noted by others. This exercise identified 48 jurisdictions from across the country. I followed the guidelines we used to determine eligibility for the City Parks Forum program; namely, the jurisdiction's population ranged from 100,000 to 800,000, which the project's funders identified as a criterion that would capture the greatest number of cities with park systems but exclude the largest cities in the U.S., which have circumstances that do not always provide a good fit as models for PAS subscribers in terms of experience, funding, staffing, and political circumstances.

My first step was to contact each community regarding their parks and open space planning efforts, in order to identify for further examination those cities or city/county governments that had a stand-alone parks and open space system plan. This exercise reduced the list to 27. We eliminated 21 jurisdictions because they: 1) did not have a comprehensive parks plan; 2) were in the process of updating their plan and, therefore, could not give us "final" plans to review; 3) had a plan in the draft stage and not officially approved; and 4) had plans for key park resources, but not the entire park and open space system.

I reviewed these 27 plans and created a matrix to compare them, using 26 different criteria. The matrix is shown in Appendix B of this PAS Report. Based upon the comparison, this list of plans was narrowed down further to include only those plans produced within the last five years because many plans have a five-year implementation schedule. The other criteria considered plans that: made strong connections to other planning documents, reports, or legislation; used a standards approach customized for local needs and conditions; or used or created a broader definition of parks. I also included plans that employed or suggested innovative funding approaches.

This process ultimately identified nine plans that I examine in detail and profile for this report:

- Alexandria, Virginia's, Open Space Plan
- Bellevue, Washington's, Parks and Open Space System Plan
- Denver, Colorado's, Game Plan: Creating a Strategy for the Future
- Eugene, Oregon's, Parks, Recreation, and Open Space (PROS) Comprehensive Plan
- Indianapolis/Marion County, Indiana's, Park, Recreation, and Open Space Plan
- Nashville/Davidson County, Tennessee's, Metropolitan Parks and Greenways Master Plan
- Portland, Oregon's, Parks 2020 Vision
- Seattle, Washington's, Parks and Recreation Plan 2000
- Virginia Beach, Virginia's, Virginia Beach Outdoors Plan 2000

The comparative matrix of these plans is included in Appendix B of this PAS Report. It is important to note that this matrix is not exhaustive of all possible topics and could be expanded. While I do not analyze all the data included in the matrix in this chapter, the matrix has been included to help others create a body of literature on the topic of parks and open space plans. In addition, the list is not exhaustive; other exemplary plans obviously exist, and APA and the Planning Advisory Service would welcome feedback from our members, subscribers, and readers to further expand this catalogue.

The analysis presented here covers four areas: stakeholder participation, planning process, plan structure, and some of the specific elements addressed in the other chapters of this PAS report.

Stakeholder Participation

The foundation of most planning processes is the design and execution of a meaningful and constructive public involvement process. Chapter 3 of this report discusses the many possible forms of public involvement in the needs assessment process. Most of the plans reviewed had an extensive public participation program; in a few cases, the public participation element was not as thorough as the processes outlined in Chapter 3 because the plan was an update of a previous plan, and public "guidance" was drawn from the earlier, more thorough planning process. All the plans included information about the public processes used to develop the plan. The most commonly used technique was public surveys, followed by public meetings or forums, steering committees, and focus groups (see the comparative matrix for more information on each city's participation approaches). Most public involvement processes occurred between one and two years, including information gathering and analysis.

For all the plans, the public involvement processes were vital to create the vision, to frame issues, to inform the Level of Service (LOS) standard, and to guide the plan to completion.

Alexandria held a one-day Open Space Summit with approximately 150 participants to develop the vision for the plan. They had a keynote speaker discuss the importance of open space, and key political leaders attended to talk about open space in Alexandria. Participants then split up into breakout groups, where they brainstormed about their visions for Alexandria's open space future. The consultant who lead the planning process said the Open Space Summit resulted in "great thoughts and overlapping views," which resulted in forming the "heart of the plan." Prior to the summit, an open space steering committee was formed, which met monthly from the beginning to address various tasks, including developing a definition of open space for Alexandria and planning for the summit. This group continued to meet after the summit to help identify priorities for the plan, and they presently meet to focus on implementation.

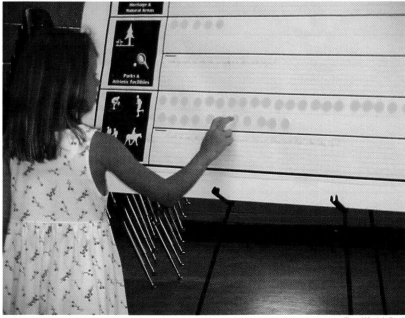

City of Virginia Beach

The design and execution of a successful planning process means meaningful citizen involvement. A young woman in Virginia Beach, Virginia, takes her first steps in civic involvement.

Denver created the Gameplan website (www.denvergov.org/gameplan), an interactive public involvement forum located on a subpage of the park department's website, which provided information to the public and provided a forum for receiving feedback. Copies of the plan can be downloaded from the website.

Eugene created a Speakers Bureau, comprised of parks department staff that made 44 presentations to community groups and organizations. These 15-minute PowerPoint presentations explained the planning process and gave participants more information about opportunities for public involvement. Staff distributed questionnaires at these events and had a nearly 70 percent response rate.

Virginia Beach created "Involving Our Citizens," a campaign that included focus groups, telephone surveys, and public meetings. The planners created a "Citizen's Choice" board, which was provided at public meetings to allow people to vote on what they felt was the top priority in their area from among four options: 1) greenways, beaches, and scenic waterways; 2) cultural and natural areas; 3) parks and athletic facilities; and 4) trails.One point to keep in mind: As noted in Chapter 3, if a survey is used to obtain public input, make sure that the survey instrument asks the questions that need to be answered. If residents are not asked about access to nature and are instead only asked about number of ball fields in their neighborhood, the basis for a park plan will be biased to favor that "quantitative" result. When reviewing the information gleaned from the various surveys, I noticed the majority of them showed the public consistently ranked natural areas, open space, and trails as the most highly desired elements of a park system. If the question about access to nature is not asked, a plan will not address such access as priority.

The Planning Process

When reviewing the plans, I noticed that each plan had a slightly different take on the specific process to use. In general, each seemed to follow a general four-step pattern.

- *Inventory and Needs Assessment*: identify community needs through an inventory of resources, public involvement processes, and community and demographic profiles

- *Vision*: create and confirm a future vision, often with a task force or committee of stakeholders

- *Goals, Objectives, and Actions*: develop strategies and a detailed plan of action. Goals may be simple or complex concepts, and may include numerous subgoals under each goal.

- *Approval and Adoption*: obtain approval for the plan from city council or appropriate governing body.

Figure 4-1, from the Eugene, Oregon, Parks, Recreation and Open Space Comprehensive Plan, shows these steps.

FIGURE 4-1. PHASES OF THE PARKS/ RECREATION/OPEN SPACE PLANNING PROCESS, EUGENE, OREGON

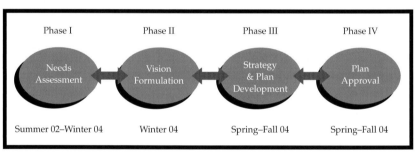

Source: Eugene, Oregon, Parks, Recreation and Open Space Comprehensive Plan

As mentioned above, each plan took a slightly different approach for each of these steps. The discussion below examines how some of the plans tailored the process to their unique circumstances.

Inventory and needs assessment. Most plans included an inventory of their parks and open space systems, but the level of detail varied. Seattle did not include an inventory as part of the plan, but rather as a separate report, the 2001 Gap Analysis Report, prepared after the plan was adopted by the city council. This was updated with a 2006 Gap Analysis Report to monitor the progress the city had made since 2001 and to better understand which areas of the city still do not meet Usable Open Space goals. The update also uses 2000 Census data, which were not available for the 2001 report, to provide more information about Seattle's population-based open space goals.

Portland included its inventory in an appendix rather than in the body of the plan. Alexandria's plan included a detailed inventory in an appendix and provided a map of open space resources along with a summary table in the main document. On the other hand, the Nashville plan assessed each park according to its open space classification, and it provided total park acreage for each park type by planning area. This level of detail allowed an extensive analysis of the condition of the existing resources.

Conducting an inventory of the amount of open space in each planning area and presenting it in the plan is helpful to understand the system, especially to understand the distribution of parks and to establish a baseline for the quantifiable side of a needs assessment. More discussion on the needs assessment portion of the plans is included later in this chapter.

Vision. In all planning processes, a visioning process provides stakeholders a starting point for participation and gives the planning process a foundation upon which to proceed. Most plans created a vision and included a vision statement in the plan.

For example, Portland's plan includes the following vision statement:

> Portland's parks, public places, natural areas and recreation opportunities give life and beauty to our city. These essential assets connect people to place, self and others. Portland's residents will treasure and care for this legacy, building on the past to provide for future generations.

Another example, from Eugene's plan:

> We envision an interconnected and accessible system of vibrant public spaces, friendly neighborhood parks, thriving natural areas and diverse recreation opportunities that make our city a healthy, active, and beautiful place in which to live, work, and play.

In addition to a vision statement, the Virginia Beach plan also included visions for each open space resource. As with its inventory, Alexandria's plan used a map to show the physical vision for the future parks and open space system; however, it did not include a written statement. The Bellevue plan used a simple idea of "city in a park" as its vision statement but described what this meant for Bellevue in great detail in the plan introduction. Similarly, Denver's plan did not include a vision statement explicitly, but rather used the first chapter of the plan to set out an extensive vision for the entire plan.

Presenting the vision as an "easily digestible" statement helps to orient the process toward the specific goals to be achieved. The plan, using the vision as a base, may emphasize conservation, facility upgrade, or system expansion. Elaborating further on the vision through either visual representation or a description of the vision as it relates to the current inventory of resources takes the vision one step further to shaping the plan's outcomes.

Goals, objectives, and actions. Every plan had a set of goals and objectives. Some minor variations in terms occurred—Bellevue simply called them objectives, and Indianapolis/Marion County called them priorities, for example—and, in addition to goals, Portland had seven "guiding principles," which are considered timeless criteria as opposed to the goals of the plan. As with any planning process, these components ensure that the information gathering, public involvement, and plan vision are translated into tangible, achievable outcomes. The number of goals varied widely—Virginia Beach had just three; Alexandria had 15. The most common number of goals was five (Nashville, Portland, and Bellevue). Indianapolis had short statements for their six priorities: Sustainability and Environmental Education; Stewardship; Cultural Legacy; Mission Driven Services; Fitness and Health; and Accessibility. Created for their original 1993 plan and used again for the 2000 plan, Seattle has seven "qualities": habitat, happiness, harmony, health, heritage, hospitality, and humanity, which represent values and long-term goals. Planners in Seattle note that they currently refer more in their efforts

STATEWIDE COMPREHENSIVE OUTDOOR RECREATION PLANS

Passed in 1965, the Land and Water Conservation Fund was established to assist states in planning, acquiring, and developing recreation resources, and to finance new federal park and recreation lands. A matching grant program was created for state and local governments to expand their outdoor resources. To qualify for the grant funds, each state was required to prepare a Statewide Comprehensive Outdoor Recreation Plan (SCORP), to be updated every five years. According to Joel Lynch, who spoke at the Federal Highway Administration's 2003 State Trails Administrator Meeting, the SCORP "is intended to describe the 'state' of outdoor recreation opportunities, demands, (both met and unmet) and outline its priorities/strategy to meet the needs of its citizens both now and in the future. Its also requires that the public have an important role in deterring the state's priorities."

The National Park Service administers the program, which is currently funded to 2015. The state agencies that oversee SCORP vary. While the SCORP inventory for each state includes all the recreation resources, the program does not have a strong connection to local park system planning. Rather, its emphasis is on providing recreation facilities and administering grants to help develop and maintain those facilities. Communities should still be aware of the SCORP for their state when preparing a local plan to ensure that planning efforts are consistent with the statewide plan.

to their overall mission statement and the mayor's goals than the "7 H's," showing once again how plans and their implementation change over time. Clearly, the 7 H's may not play a part in the plan's next update.

Actions were also included in all the plans. As with other planning processes, the actions were typically tied to specific goals and objectives. Denver did it differently; it organized its actions according to four "values" in the comprehensive plan: sustainability, equity, engagement, and sound economics. Typically, the plans had numerous actions for each objective. For example, Indianapolis had 65 defined "action steps" organized according to their six "priorities." Planners in Indianapolis note that actions not completed are rolled over to the next plan.

Plans did vary in how they organized the actions. Virginia Beach called them recommendations and organized them for each of the planning areas and for each of the resource types. Bellevue organized them according to the nine "focus areas" of the plan, which covered specific resources, such as greenways, waterfront access, and neighborhood sites, and specific issues, including partnership opportunities, and renovation, maintenance, and security.

Two observations are important here. First, not all plans translated actions into explicit implementation strategies. Some listed all the actions to be achieved, but specific priorities or implementation phases were not defined. Among the plans that stood out for their connection between the goals and implementation include Alexandria, which used results from their Open Space Summit to identify their 11 priority actions; Bellevue, which had short- and long-term capital recommendations by focus area (looking at specific resources and issues); Eugene, which had a separate Project and Priority Action Plan, the result of a two-year public input process that identified the proposed projects and their priority levels; and Virginia Beach, with its recommendations ranked as high, medium, or low priorities. Portland and Indianapolis use the capital improvements plan as their implementation mechanism for specific projects.

Second, there was not always consistency across the plans in the use of the terms "goals, objectives, and actions." As noted above, some plans used the terms "values" or "principles" for goals; and "priorities" or "recommendations" for actions. This variation made it somewhat difficult to analyze across the plans, especially in instances where there appeared to be other organizing elements in addition to the goals; sometimes goals were stated, but then the actions were based on "strategy areas" or "values." The plans that included simple goal statements, more detailed objectives under each goal, and actions translated into priorities to achieve specific objectives were the documents easiest to review and understand.

Approval and adoption. Interestingly, not all of the plans reviewed explicitly noted if the city council or other governing body officially adopted the plan. Of the nine plans, only four made specific reference to a resolution. Virginia Beach went one step further; in addition to accepting the plan as a guidance document for open space and recreation planning, it also stated that it would be integrated as part of the city's next comprehensive plan. Indeed, the city's 2003 comprehensive plan references the 2000 Outdoors Plan, and much of the relevant information in the comprehensive plan's technical document is from the 2000 Outdoors Plan. In addition, the 2007 Outdoors Plan (under development at the time of this writing) will be part of the city's 2008 Comprehensive Plan in a similar manner.

As noted at the beginning of this chapter, the park department or commission and the governing body should officially adopt the plan to ensure that it becomes a binding document for staff and the decision makers. It also ensures

Not all plans translated actions into explicit implementation strategies. Some listed all the actions to be achieved, but specific priorities or implementation phases were not defined.

consistency with other planning efforts, helps to avoid duplicate planning efforts, and provides a key reference point for the comprehensive plan.

Plan Structure

In addition to reviewing the plan process, I also reviewed their structure. Most of the cities used the process as the framework for their structure. The typical table of contents included the following items:

- Executive Summary
- Introduction (varied in content and detail; see comparative matrix for different approaches)
- Current state of the system (history, previous planning efforts, inventory, issues, park system definition)
- Needs Assessment (trends, level of service, public input process and results)
- Plan for System (including goals, objectives, and actions)
- Implementation (short- and long-term priorities)
- Funding sources
- Evaluation (annual reports; plan updates on website; indicators and performance measures)

As mentioned above, the plan structure in many cases mirrors the planning process; the analysis here looks at how the plans used the executive summary, introduction, and evaluation sections.

The Executive Summary. A majority of the plans included an executive summary. Providing an executive summary gives the reader a "snapshot" of all the plan's key elements—plan purpose, state of the park system, vision, actions, implementation strategies, and funding. Denver's executive summary presented this information as a summary of each chapter. Nashville's presented a quick digest of the existing system, proposals, and estimated costs.

Some used the executive summary to focus on the priorities; Portland summarized the six specific actions to be taken over the next 20 years and the recommended strategies to best implement them.

Because comprehensive parks and open space plans involve extensive amounts of data gathering and analysis, plans should provide a summary of the plan conclusions and outcomes at the beginning of the document.

Because comprehensive parks and open space plans involve extensive amounts of data gathering and analysis, plans should provide a summary of the plan conclusions and outcomes at the beginning of the document. Such a summary makes it much easier to demonstrate to readers that the plan is the result of a process with definable outcomes and allows the reader to see these outcomes without having to work to extract them from the larger document.

The Introduction. Nearly all the plans included an introduction. For most of the plans, this section was the place to discuss the purpose of this plan and the planning process, including stakeholder involvement. Alexandria and Indianapolis used the introduction to provide a history of the community in relation to parks; Bellevue and Portland used it to elaborate the vision for the park system.

For the Seattle plan, the introduction described the connection the plan had to other planning efforts, especially the 1994 Seattle comprehensive plan and the various neighborhood plans. It also gave the context for this plan with respect to previous park planning efforts, noting that this was an update to the 1993 parks plan. Seattle adopted a new comprehensive plan in 2005, and while the parks department had hoped to prepare a new plan in light of issues raised in the new comprehensive plan, city leaders have asked the department to develop a strategic plan that focuses on lines of business, priorities for funding, and how to make choices in a world of limited funding.

This example raises an important point: the connection that a park system plan has to other planning efforts. All but one of the plans referenced the variety of plans in their communities that had a connection to park planning; in nearly every case, this included a connection between the comprehensive plan and the park plan. For Alexandria and Eugene, the comprehensive plan is the basis for the parks and open space system plan, with the comprehensive plan's parks and open space element serving as the foundation. Alexandria adopted their plan as part of the community's comprehensive plan, and it will be updated as the comprehensive plan is updated. As mentioned above, for Virginia Beach, the park system plan is an update to a previous parks plan and will inform the next comprehensive planning effort.

Plans for other resources that have a relationship to parks should be reviewed and understood to inform the inventory and needs assessment, and to ensure that the park system plan does not duplicate efforts. For example, Indianapolis and Nashville have greenway plans separate from the parks and open space system plan. Denver and Seattle have separate plans for pedestrian paths and bikeways, which, like greenways, are complementary to parks and open spaces. In addition, other myriad community elements intersect with parks, like housing, downtowns, and neighborhoods, which Bellevue, Denver, Indianapolis, and Seattle all mention as related to parks.

Bellevue includes a list of all related plans in an appendix to its parks plans and notes them throughout the document as well. Of particular note is the connection the Bellevue plan makes to the capital improvements plan (CIP). In addition to the plan noting that the CIP is connected to the parks plan, the specific connection is made throughout the parks plan, so as to not duplicate efforts.

Making reference to the relationship to other plans at the relevant places in the parks plan is useful. It helps to make the connection between the plans more clear than simply listing them in an appendix or in the introduction, and specific relationships, such as the role that a separate greenway plan has to the system plan, can be discussed. However, plans should also provide a full list of all the related plans at some place in the park system plan. This is helpful in understanding what other planning efforts are related to parks planning, and if these efforts are being coordinated.

Evaluation. Most of the plans did mention a method of evaluating plan implementation. For example, the Bellevue plan devoted a chapter to reviewing the projects completed and progress made since the previous plan (1993) was adopted. With regard to how the current plan would be evaluated, two approaches were generally used: actual evaluation mechanisms or methods of reporting to the public the activities to date.

Two of the plans mention that an indicators and performance goals approach will be used to measure progress. For Denver, their indicators system will use the current status of the park system as the benchmark upon which the indicators (to address each of the 10 goal items) will be measured. Denver has not yet adopted an indicators system to monitor the plan, but staff hopes that the planning unit within the parks department will institutionalize a monitoring system that will be used for all strategic planning and the annual budget process. Eugene also intends to use a performance measures approach, and updates will be made available on the departmental website. Eugene anticipates it will begin to report their performance measures in spring 2007.

Nashville currently uses its departmental website to provide plan updates. Their website is updated as needed with news of meetings for community

Plans for other resources that have a relationship to parks should be reviewed and understood to inform the inventory and needs assessment, and to ensure that the park system plan does not duplicate efforts.

input or to reveal architectural renderings, or ceremonies for ground break-ings or facility openings, for example.

Annual reports or other regular update efforts are also used. In the past, Indianapolis has conducted an annual review and update of the action plan, capital improvements plan, and acquisition plan, as well as an annual solicitation of stakeholder input. While the current plan states that the city will continue to do this, Indianapolis park planners say they now meet more frequently with their key stakeholders—parks advisory groups, parks board, foundations, and friends organizations—to address concerns, rather than convening a large group annually. Indianapolis has also created a newsletter, which can be subscribed to on the city's website, to inform the general public of updates and activities. Virginia Beach publishes a semi-annual report each January and July to provide information on open space acquisition and funding. The most current report is available on its department website. Department staff prepares the report on behalf of the city-council-appointed open space subcommittee.

Evaluation of plan effectiveness is highly important to determine if the actions identified in the documents become realities. As with other types of planning efforts, a clear method for evaluating success needs to be defined and monitored over time. As one park planner told me, the political process can stall a plan; if a new mayor is elected and a new set of staff are appointed, this lack of continuity can put the breaks on plan evaluation until the new leadership are up to speed. A robust, institutionalized evaluation mecha-nism, however, should be able to withstand changes in leadership. And, in the ongoing climate of limited funds for park acquisition and maintenance, creating a clear and easily understood set of indicators and benchmarks makes it much easier to focus needed resources on specific items and to track the progress over time. Many communities now use indicators to track the progress of other planning efforts, such as the larger comprehensive plan, or for more specific subareas, such as neighborhoods. Parks departments should reach out to the planning department and other city agencies as well as nonprofit organizations that operate indicators projects to "piggyback" on them and to share data with them from the parks department.

Evaluation of plan effectiveness is highly important to determine if the actions identified in the documents become realities. As with other types of planning efforts, a clear method for evaluating success needs to be defined and monitored over time.

Specific Plan Elements

Because this report is called *From Recreation to Re-creation: New Directions in Parks and Open Space System Planning*, I examined the plans to see if any of them were adopting or moving in the direction of the approaches discussed in this report's other chapters. Specifically examined is the degree to which the plans:

- expand the definition of "park" (e.g., consider it as part of a larger system);
- identify the myriad benefits of parks beyond recreation—and include them in the plan;
- create a parks level of service responsive to local desires and conditions; and
- identify new and creative funding sources to achieve implementation goals.

Expanding the definition of a park. Most plans used a typical hierarchy of parks—regional, community, neighborhood, mini-parks, and special use parks—as their starting point, but some of the plans then expand in vari-ous ways. Some outstanding examples of plans that created unique park definitions follow.

Alexandria's plan defined parks in terms of five "layers":

1. primary uses (active, passive, trails, and streetscape/scenic roadways);
2. secondary characteristics (specific uses and the character of the space);
3. service area (both users and geographic areas);
4. ownership; and
5. maintenance.

Each space is thus defined by measuring how each of the five layers applies, much like a geographic information system (GIS) describes a place in terms of data layers.

Denver's "City in a Park" concept allowed them to broaden the definition of parks and open spaces to include other elements, such as community gardens, plazas, schoolyards, and nontraditional areas like rooftops (potential green spaces) and street trees. It also presented the idea of green neighborhoods, with each neighborhood having "a bit of breathing space," here defined as "safe, accessible and flexible open spaces located within a half-mile of every home." Finally, the term "recreation" is rethought in the Denver plan as "re-creation," or any place that allows someone to "re-create" oneself, which itself expands the notion of recreation beyond ball fields and basketball courts (and helped to inspire the title for this report).

Seattle's plan has four elements to its open space system:

1. Breathing Room Open Space, similar to Denver's definition but broader in that it is a combination of all dedicated open spaces except for "submerged" park lands (tidelands and shorelands).
2. Usable Open Space, which includes accessible spaces that meet certain size and physical criteria allowing for use.
3. Greenspaces, which are natural and ecologically valuable areas, including greenbelts.
4. Offsets, defined as resources that are not owned by parks and recreation but are used in the same manner as city-owned facilities. The prime example is school grounds.

One noticeable trend is the idea of identifying resources that provide similar benefits as city-owned parks and open spaces but that are perhaps under other ownership or are not traditionally included as part of a parks and open space system.

The Virginia Beach plan considers all elements to be part of an "outdoor system," which includes four components: 1) greenways, beaches, and scenic waterways; 2) cultural and natural resources; 3) parks and athletic fields; and 4) trails. Parks are defined as neighborhood, community, or district parks, and school spaces and homeowner "semi-public" parks are also included.

One noticeable trend is the idea of identifying resources that provide similar benefits as city-owned parks and open spaces but that are perhaps under other ownership or are not traditionally included as part of a parks and open space system. For example, including school facilities as part of the definition of community open space resources means they are included in the inventory and needs analysis, and the functions of these spaces are then not duplicated by the parks department. The result is the more efficient use of existing resources.

Another interesting concept is that an open space system might include places that aren't necessarily "accessible"; green roofs are a good example of that. When one considers parks as part of a larger parks and open space system—one that can provide numerous functions as described in Chapter 2—the system can then include components not traditionally considered a "park" but still planned for and protected as part of the larger system. Components like green roofs, however, should not be considered "replacements" for parks if the priority is to increase accessible public open space. Communities need to create a definition for their park system—and the components of that system—that fits the community's character, history, and priorities.

Identifying the myriad benefits of parks. All but one of the plans included information on the benefits of parks, open space, and recreation. For the most part, the plans used general information to describe the benefits. Bellevue noted the multiple uses of parks as habitat, trails, historical and cultural heritage sites, and opportunities for environmental education. Nashville's plan provided a qualitative list including recreation, water quality and stormwater management, wildlife habitat, air quality, alternative transportation, community appearance and character, and education. Seattle supported its vision statement with a narrative to note the contribution of parks and open space to the city's identity, stability, urban design, and network of public services, the well being of the citizens, and the overall health of the community and its quality of life. A few of the plans did take this discussion a step further, however, and identified some specific benefits beyond the usual array.

An example of a publicly accessible green roof, Nashville Public Square is a 7.5-acre downtown site with a 2.25-acre state-of-the-art intensive green roof over a parking structure. Developed by Hawkins Partners, Inc., this project received the 2007 "Award of Excellence" from Green Roofs for Healthy Cities (www.greenroofs.org).

Green Roofs for Healthy Cities

The Alexandria plan included specifically the benefits of greenways, as defined by the Virginia Department of Conservation and Recreation. These benefits (which in many cases could also be considered benefits of open space generally) include:

- connecting people and communities;
- providing alternative transportation routes;
- softening urban landscapes;
- enhancing economic development and tourism;
- increasing real property values;
- improving water quality; and
- improving the overall quality of life in the community.

The plan also noted the benefits of open space resources, focusing on attracting and retaining residents and businesses; the positive effects on property values, discussing the "proximate properties" principle ("attractive open space can enhance the value (and hence the tax yield) of adjacent or fronting properties by approximately 20 percent"); lower cost to government for land kept as open space rather than developed for residential uses; and the overall benefits provided as social and quality-of-life assets. The public is realizing these benefits and is supporting open space funding efforts in Virginia Beach through ballot box initiatives.

Denver's plan, which sees the community as "a city in an ecological park," takes a strong position on using parks and open space as green infrastructure; it specifically addresses ways to integrate public open space with stormwater drainage and air- and water-quality controls. It also connects open space preservation with water conservation, specifically through using climate-appropriate plantings. In addition, the plan explicitly states that parks are "economic and social catalysts for neighborhoods."

The Indianapolis plan discusses both the qualitative and quantitative benefits of parks and open space, organized under four categories:

1. Health and fitness (benefits of physical activity on public health and overall sense of well-being)

2. Environmental (water quality and quantity, air pollution control, and habitat preservation)

3. Economic (tourism, property values, attracting business and industry, and reinvestment in property)

4. Community benefits (crime reduction, social interaction, and overall quality of life).

Among the various points made to support these ideas are data from general studies, such as the potential for one shade tree to save the equivalent energy expenditure of up to four air conditioners operating all day, to studies specific to the region, like the Indiana University Purdue University at Indianapolis (IUPUI) study that found that homes in a Indianapolis greenway corridor had $3,371 in added value, and homes near the Monon Trail had $13,059 in added value (Lindsay 2003).

Portland's plan lists the benefits as part of a larger narrative about the city's park system, noting that it:

• provides tourism benefits;

• contributes to the overall quality of life (and is part of the reason for the city's high ranking on "best places to live" reports);

Denver's plan very much emphasizes using the parks system for "green infrastructure," as is shown here where stormwater is being retained in a park for later release.

- enhances urban livability by providing connections between neighborhoods and nature;
- builds community;
- provides river, trail, and habitat recreation;
- helps define the city's character;
- increases neighborhood value and desirability;
- establishes places of physical renewal; and
- links people to community resources.

The Virginia Beach plan includes a detailed section on the fiscal impact of open space to address the concern for lost revenues from forgone development on open spaces. As with the Alexandria plan, Virginia Beach looked at the positive impact open spaces have on the property values of adjacent properties, citing the work of John Crompton in *The Impact of Parks and Open Space on Property Values and the Property Tax Base* (NRPA 2000). It also evaluates the increased demand on public expenditures by residential and commercial development as compared to keeping land as open space. For this analysis, this plan had the benefit of data from a 1990 study of fiscal impacts conducted specifically for Virginia Beach (data were updated for 1999). The plan also looked at what it called "long-term benefits" of open space, including increased property values, protection of the environment, and improvements in the quality of life for citizens. This plan stands out on this particular issue because all of its points made under long-term benefits are supported by actual examples, such as property value data from other communities, studies of the specific environmental benefits of open space, such as water protection and tree preservation, and citations from other publications on the quality-of-life impacts.

There are generally three layers to the discussion of the benefits of parks:

1. The traditionally recognized benefits, such as recreation and overall quality of life
2. The more complex environmental and economic benefits, such as stormwater management, air quality improvements, and increased property values
3. The site-specific benefits, such as the information in the Indianapolis and Virginia Beach plans on specific dollar value increases to property values

As the plans go from the broader benefits to the more specific, they become more powerful. It is likely that the plans that describe site-specific, tangible benefits will capture the imagination and interest of the public and the decision makers more successfully that those that address them more broadly.

CREATING A CUSTOMIZED PARK LEVEL OF SERVICE

Chapter 3 of this report discusses the ways of designing and implementing a needs assessment, using three types of techniques: anecdotal, qualitative, and quantitative. The public involvement processes described above likely capture many of the anecdotal and qualitative information sources; here we focus on one important component of the quantitative: the LOS for parks (or often called "park standards").

Every jurisdiction's plan I reviewed used some type of LOS measurement to evaluate whether the park system was meeting current needs or able to meet projected future needs. A number of the plans used what was referred to as the "NRPA standards," which typically meant the use of exact measurements for each park type (X acres per 1,000 population). The most recent version of that document, *Park, Recreation, Open Space and Greenway Guidelines* (Mertes and Hall 1996), essentially replaced any suggestion of an

There are three layers to the discussion of the benefits of parks:

1. *Traditionally recognized benefits (e.g., recreation)*
2. *More complex environmental and economic benefits*
3. *Site-specific benefits (e.g., property value increases)*

absolute standard with location requirements, expressed in terms of distance to parks. The plans typically use both of these metrics as a "one-two" approach to planning for parks: use the NRPA "standards" and benchmarks from other cities as the first basis for providing parks, and then refine this with an assessment based on distance, which allows communities to more accurately assess access to parks. This could also be thought of as first taking a "macro" look at parks (provision of parks acreage in the city overall) and then reevaluating with a "micro" look at actual level of service by accessibility. Here are some examples of how the plans used standards and level of service.

Bellevue's plan initially based its park needs on a set of NRPA open space standards but then discussed the limitations of those standards, and subsequently modified them in terms of service area and park size. The plan states an ultimate goal of providing a park within one-half mile of every citizen. It also discusses meeting the needs of special populations, including youth, seniors, ethnic groups, and the disabled, which further indicates how applying a uniform standard does not work to meet all the varying open space needs in a community.

The Denver plan presents an LOS unique to Denver, based on four considerations: 1) comparison cities as benchmarks; 2) expertise within the parks department; 3) NRPA standards; and 4) resident surveys. Their standards are expressed as performance goals, such as providing a tree canopy cover of 15 to 18 percent in residential areas by 2025, and providing at least one-half acre of public open space within one-half mile of every resident's home that can be reached wi thout crossing a major barrier. To support this approach, they cite Minneapolis and Seattle as other cities that use "access" as an LOS measurement. Interestingly, they exclude golf courses from final LOS evaluation for open space because, while they are public facilities, they are not "public" in that residents are not free to just visit them. Also, because they are an enterprise fund item (that is, they receive funds from an account separate from the general fund, and costs are financed primarily through user fees) and have a revenue system quite different from the rest of the park system, they are treated differently from other system components.

Eugene's plan used a general standard of 20 acres per 1,000 people for all open space, based on national figures and local needs. Similar to Denver, however, Eugene also addressed needs in terms of distance to parks. This plan uses different distances depending upon the type of park discussed. For example, one-half mile is the recommended distance to a neighborhood park (defined here as a minimum of four acres and including children's play equipment, unprogrammed outdoor space, accessible pathways, and other features), and two miles is recommended for community parks (defined here as a minimum of 40 acres in size, and in addition to neighborhood park features also including picnic areas, gathering spaces, pathways and trails, and parking and access to transit).

The Indianapolis plan uses a LOS based primarily on service area for three park types: between one-half mile and three miles to a community park; between one-quarter and one-half mile to a neighborhood park, and between several blocks or less than one-quarter mile to a minipark (between 2,500 square feet and one acre in size).

Similar to the above plans, Nashville's plan also uses both a standard and an LOS related to distance. But this plan also includes an LOS standard for greenways, defined as two miles. It also looks at parkland as a percentage of the total land area in the community. The city's needs assessment defined the open space needs according to four terms:

1. Expressed (the resource already exists)

2. Latent (the need exists but is not yet being met)

3. Comparative (other communities address the need)

4. Normative (standards)

Of all the plans, however, Seattle's plan presented the most detailed LOS system. Called Distribution Guidelines, the plan presents a desirable LOS for each resource, an acceptable LOS, and a description of "offsets," as mentioned above. For example, for Breathing Room Open Space, the desirable LOS is one acre per 100 population; the acceptable LOS is one-third acre per 100 residents; and the offsets include school grounds, green streets, boulevards, and trails. This LOS was then applied to each planning sector to identify where gaps exist (and the city generated maps of the sectors showing these gaps and included them in the plan).

For all the plans, there is a definite benefit to using general LOS standards, either from a national source or other similar communities: it gives those preparing the plans a starting point for creating local standards. Too many plans in the past, however, have used outmoded—and untested—data as the absolute. Using the alternative of LOS based on distance from residences, and then generating a "gap analysis" from this LOS, appears to be a better way to create a set of criteria to fit local needs. Communities will be better served to use general standards or LOS to begin discussions with stakeholders but then allow input from stakeholders to truly customize the standards to meet local conditions.

IDENTIFYING NEW AND CREATIVE FUNDING SOURCES

Most plans included a description of the current revenue sources for parks. In general, these funding sources were what one would expect, including the general fund, bonds, taxes, capital improvements funding, and user fees. But some plans noted less-dependable sources, namely grants and donations. And still other plans described potential sources of funding that could result in more permanent revenue streams.

The Eugene plan proposes a number of potential revenue sources from other tax systems other than property taxes to be pursued, specifically entertainment, utility, corporate income, income tax surcharge, personal income, gross receipts, payroll, general sales, restaurant, business license, and new construction fees. The plan also suggests the creation of a special district, which would have its own tax base to fund projects, rather than trying to get its share of the property tax revenues. The plan notes, however, that several procedural steps would be involved in creating the district and that getting public buy-in might be difficult. In fact, discussions with the current parks and open space planning manager indicate that neither the alternative tax revenue sources nor the special district have been successfully achieved.

Denver's plan includes a table listing capital projects, estimated costs, and potential funding sources. The issues faced in Denver are a high dependence on the general fund for operating costs and the constraints that the Taxpayers' Bill of Rights (TABOR) puts on the use of those revenues. Plan preparers recognize that partnerships and increased efficiencies cannot address all the shortfalls, and they use a "willingness to pay" survey to determine the tax increase the public would support for parks.

An alternative source is being considered for park funding, however. Denver is still recovering from a long-term drought and municipal financial cutbacks that have hurt park funding. An increase in funding is needed to combat the drought and its effect on park property, so the plan's infrastructure needs assessments have been used to prepare a bond issue to bolster park funding.

Among the current sources of funds and land outlined in Portland's plan are the general fund, federal and state grants, donations, and the residential systems development charge (an impact fee). Potential sources listed include

For all the plans, there is a definite benefit to using general LOS standards, either from a national source or other similar communities: it gives those preparing the plans a starting point for creating local standards.

general obligation bonds (used successfully in the past), regional funding (from Metro, the regional government), niche taxes (e.g., a restaurant tax), and a nonresidential development impact fee. While Portland does not currently impose a niche tax for parks funding, it has received funds from Metro for land acquisition, and the city council has asked the parks department to develop a method for a nonresidential development impact fee for the council's consideration. And within the last five to six years, tax increment financing (TIF) funds have been a source of funding land acquisition and park development within Portland's urban renewal areas.

Among the traditional funding sources identified in Virginia Beach's plan are bonds, pay-as-you-go fees (essentially user fees), and a tax increase (proposed as $60 per year per household). An innovative idea in the plan is to create a designated fund for open space acquisition. Correspondence with the park planning staff indicated that, while past acquisitions were made from a variety of funding sources, a portion of the city's meals and restaurant tax funds now are the primary source of revenues for current acquisitions. In addition, the city is evaluating the feasibility of establishing a dedicated funding source to extend its open space acquisition program into the future.

In general, while the plans often propose an innovative or alternative mechanism to fund parks, rarely do these become a reality. And as Chapter 5 points out, the traditional funding mechanisms are more commonly applied to parkland acquisition and other capital items, and not to fund ongoing maintenance and operations. So the challenge remains to find ways to keep park systems viable and successful long after a parks plan is adopted.

CONCLUSION

Access to parks is a common challenge for communities.

When stepping back and looking at all of the park plans I reviewed, some common themes became apparent, especially ones that reinforce many of the ideas in other chapters of this report.

- *Access to parks is a common challenge for communities.* The problem may be one of equity—a community may be perceived to be "well parked," but the reality is that the distribution of parks is not equitable across the community, and goals (e.g., providing open space within one-half mile of each residence) still need to be met.

- *Barriers to parks are an access issue.* Residents of a neighborhood may have a park within a certain distance, but it cannot be accessed due to physical or other barriers. The solution may be to removing the barrier, or if that is not feasible, other open space resources may need to be provided. In addition, disabled residents may not be able to easily access a park and enjoy its benefits. The principles of universal design, which works to make environments and products accessible for use by as many people as possible regardless of their ability level, provide one approach to addressing this problem. For more information on universal design, see The Center for Universal Design at North Carolina State University, http://www.design.ncsu.edu/cud/index.htm.

- *Parks are often seen as opportunities to make connections and links in communities, for transportation, green infrastructure, or other reasons.* This perspective reinforces the idea of a park system rather than just a collection of open spaces. Such an approach can be the organizing principle for a plan, as was the case in Denver.

- *Communities have other resources that can provide similar services as parks do, especially in terms of recreation, and these resources should be included in the parks needs analysis.* School resources are now commonly included as part of the "offsets" that should be considered in a needs assessment. Communities may also consider private recreation providers in this assessment, which may reduce the recreation demand on public facilities. This approach can reduce the pressure to make every park or facility meet all the desired goals.

- *Residents are increasingly interested in "nonorganized" activities in their parks, seeking connections to nature and access to open space for its intrinsic benefits.* This helps communities reframe "recreation" to become "re-creation," and provide places for people to re-create themselves. While recreation fields are still desired, park plans are shifting their focus to also address environmental stewardship and natural resource protection to conserve these areas. Stakeholder participation must be designed to capture information about these broader interests.

- *"Green" elements sometimes extend beyond parks and open spaces, but they are still addressed as part of the system.* Plans often spoke of "green streets," which might simply encompass an increased street tree canopy but could be expanded to include sidewalks, bikeways, or boulevards to provide connectors to parks and other destinations in a more "green" manner, or they could also be environmentally designed streets to provide stormwater management through drainage and plantings. Green issues also came up in the form of water issues, specifically water conservation in arid climates and stormwater management

- *Communities are becoming more creative in their definition of open space.* Places are seeing opportunities to increase their inventory not only through the conversion of vacant urban land, but also in new venues like rooftops. Along with the inclusion of other "green" resources, this allows communities to adopt more encompassing terms for these resources, like "breathing space," which serves to capture many of the additional functions and services of parks but also provides for a more rigorous level of service to be used.

- *Communities that prepare comprehensive parks and open space plans look at their park systems broadly for the entire jurisdiction, but then consider specific needs—and recommendations to meet those needs—on a subarea basis.* The subareas most often coincide with the planning subareas, typically neighborhoods.

- *In addition to neighborhoods, downtown is increasingly seen as a place for more parks.* This may be related to understanding the positive effect that parks have on business attraction and retention, tourism revenues, and other economic benefits.

- *Plans are using approaches and technology from land-use planning to measure progress toward their goals.* The Nashville plan uses a type of "shift-share" analysis, called the index of participation, resulting in a comparison of statewide recreation trends with national trends to develop a "significance value" for a particular need. This measurement helps determine priorities. Benchmarks, performance goals, and indicators—used in neighborhood planning for several years—are now migrating over to park planning. And GIS is commonly used to spatially represent park data.

Thus overall, park plans are beginning to resemble comprehensive plans, addressing numerous, complex issues and their connection. In the 1970s, it appeared that recreation services were what the public desired from parks, but today's stakeholders are interested in much broader, less-well-defined benefits, and the plans are reflecting this. As the definition of park becomes even broader, park system plans will need to continue to evolve.

Residents are increasingly interested in "nonorganized" activities in their parks, seeking connections to nature and access to open space for its intrinsic benefits.

CHAPTER 4 REFERENCES

Crompton, John L. 2000. *The Impact of Parks and Open Space on Property Values and the Property Tax Base*. Arlington, Va.: National Recreation and Park Association.

Harnik, Peter. 2000. *Inside City Parks*. Washington, DC: Urban Land Institute.

Lindsey, Greg, Seth Payton, Joyce Man, and John Ottensmann. 2003. *Public Choices and Property Values: Evidence from Greenways in Indianapolis*. Indianapolis: IUPUI Center for Urban Policy and the Environment. http://www.urbancenter.iupui .edu/PubResources/pdf/44_03-C19.1_Greenway.pdf (8/15/07).

Mertes, James D. and James R. Hall. 1996. *Park, Recreation, Open Space and Greenway Guidelines*. Arlington, Va.: National Recreation and Park Association.

Websites of Cities and Jurisdictions Included in the Analysis
(Please also See Appendix B)

Alexandria, Virginia: http://alexandriava.gov/recreation/general/OpenSpacehome .html

Bellevue, Washington: http://www.ci.bellevue.wa.us/pdf/Parks/2003%20Bellevue,% 20WA%20Park%20Plan.pdf

Denver, Colorado: http://www.denvergov.org/gameplan/

Eugene, Oregon: (www.eugene-or.gov/portal/server.pt?space=CommunityPage& cached=true&parentname=CommunityPage&parentid=0&in_hi_userid =2&control =SetCommunity&CommunityID=217&PageID=1360)

Indianapolis/Marion Co, Indiana: www.indygov.org/eGov/City/DPR/Admin/ Planning/home.htm

Nashville, Tennessee: www.nashville.gov/parks/master_plan.htm

Portland, Oregon: http://www.portlandonline.com/parks/index.cfm?c=eabic

Seattle, Washington: http://www.seattle.gov/parks/publications/developmentplan .htm

Virginia Beach, Virginia: www.vbgov.com/dept/parks/design/0,1457,2101,00.html

CHAPTER 5

Creating and Maintaining Parks:
Funding and Other Means

By Peter Harnik

Traditionally, cities created parks, either on greenfield sites or sites previously occupied by another use, through a five-stage process:

1. A park location is identified through a planning process.
2. The city council, using normal municipal funds, authorizes a financial appropriation.
3. The department of parks and recreation purchases the land.
4. The department of parks and recreation, using its normal budgetary appropriation for capital improvements, develops the land into a park.
5. The department of parks and recreation, using its normal budgetary appropriation for ongoing operations, maintains the park.

This is the ideal process, but, in fact, probably fewer than 50 percent of all new urban parks come about in this way today. The fact is that few cities have a sufficiently stable funding base or political decision-making stream to follow this protocol. The process is frequently upended and then occasionally restored by one or more remedies—which is why the history of the creation of so many parks reads like a chapter from *The Perils of Pauline*.

The most common challenge is insufficient funding for park acquisition and development in the park department's budget. The most common remedies include finding alternative public revenue sources, requiring developer donations, offering benefits in exchange for developer donations, and soliciting private donations. The most difficult remedy to find is an alternative funding source for ongoing park maintenance if the park department's budget is too small.

Based on research by the Center for City Park Excellence (CCPE), it appears that a park department needs an annual total budget (i.e., operations plus capital) of at least $85 to $95 per resident to have a sufficient funding base to adequately run the system and to also create new parks. Seattle, San Francisco, Minneapolis, Chicago, and Kansas City, among other cities, are in this higher-spending group (see Table 5-1). One reason for the fiscal strength of the park departments in Chicago, Kansas City, and Minneapolis is that each receives its funding directly from the property tax rather than through an appropriation from the city council. This structure, which requires an amendment to the city charter, is difficult to pass but helps shield the department from annual political budget vagaries and improves the ability to do long-range planning and acquisition. But since the majority of park agencies do not get their funding this way, most of them need alternative mechanisms to achieve their goals.

If no money is initially available to buy a property, three possible remedies exist: getting the land for free, finding an alternative public agency buyer, or generating more revenue.

GETTING LAND FOR FREE

There are five mechanisms to obtaining park land for free: donations by developers, donations by philanthropists, mitigations and legal settlements, interagency transfer, and tax-defaulted properties.

Donations by Developers

It may be possible to strike a deal with a property's developer to set aside some land for a park. Many locales have a "developer impact fee" (also called "developer exaction ordinance," "system development charge," or other similar term) that mandates a "set-aside" of land for a park (or a payment to the city to purchase such land) to mitigate the impact of population growth; in other places, the process is handled in informal negotiations that usually involve granting the developer a density bonus in return for the donation of land or money. In Chicago, developers occasionally agree to provide funds not only for park acquisition but also for maintenance. In some cases, the corporate landowner is an extractive industry (timber or mining company) that has already gotten all of its value out of the land and is willing to donate the whole property. In Sacramento, Granite Regional Park came about through a donation from a sand-and-gravel mining operation after the excavation work was completed. (As an additional benefit, the park is valued for its sinuous contours in an otherwise flat landscape.)

Another way of gaining parkland— unusual but not unheard of—is as mitigation for the loss of other lands.

Donations by Philanthropists

Alternatively, it may be possible to convince a wealthy individual or a private foundation to donate a property as a park. The gift can be made directly to the government or through the use of a third-party nonprofit organization; in either case, the donor receives a tax deduction for his or her generosity. Some donors—particularly those leaving the land as a bequest—feel more comfortable using a land conservancy, which then donates the property to the city. They feel that the conservancy can help make sure that the land is not misused, traded away, or sold off in the future. (One way of protecting it is to place a conservation easement on the property, preventing it from being developed, although some cities will not accept a property with many legal restrictions on it.)

Mitigation and Legal Settlements

Another way of gaining parkland—unusual but not unheard of—is as mitigation for the loss of other lands. In Tampa, Florida, in the 1980s the city needed to dredge a channel in Tampa Bay, but doing so resulted in the generation of a large amount of sand and mud that was dumped on wetlands. In compensation for the destruction of the wetlands, the port authority agreed to buy up other private wetlands and put them into permanent protected status as parkland.

On rare occasions, cities are lucky enough to acquire parkland as a result of some corporate malfeasance punished in a court of law. In 1982, the Unocal Corporation, a California oil company, was found guilty of polluting San Francisco Bay and killing thousands of birds and wildlife with chemical

TABLE 5-1. TOTAL PARK-RELATED EXPENDITURE PER RESIDENT, SELECTED CITIES (DATA FROM FISCAL YEAR 2004)

CITY	POPULATION	TOTAL PARK EXPENDITURE	EXPENDITURE PER RESIDENT
Washington, D.C.	553,523	$146,250,104	$264
Seattle	572,475	$136,369,421	$238
Cincinnati	314,154	$52,175,643	$166
Chicago	2,862,244	$465,515,116	$163
Minneapolis	373,943	$54,054,637	$145
Tampa	321,772	$43,095,235	$134
San Jose	904,522	$111,460,086	$123
Kansas City, Mo.	444,387	$54,605,149	$123
Portland, Ore.	533,492	$64,209,345	$120
Sacramento	454,330	$53,393,206	$118
Long Beach	476,564	$54,356,905	$114
Denver	556,835	$62,764,158	$113
Tucson	512,023	$54,391,620	$106
San Diego	1,263,756	$132,106,294	$105
Colorado Springs	369,363	$33,802,924	$92
Phoenix	1,418,041	$125,745,488	$89
Atlanta	419,122	$35,979,371	$86
Boston	569,165	$47,940,409	$84
Columbus, Ohio	730,008	$60,018,919	$82
New York	8,104,079	$635,753,000	$78
Oakland	397,976	$29,271,558	$74
Nashville/Davidson County	572,475	$42,030,405	$73
Jacksonville	777,704	$50,029,762	$64
Albuquerque	484,246	$28,593,026	$59
Miami	379,724	$22,329,585	$59
St. Louis	343,279	$19,998,140	$58
Dallas	1,210,393	$68,198,817	$56
Fort Worth	603,337	$33,001,171	$55
Mesa	437,454	$23,378,119	$53
San Antonio	1,236,249	$63,765,209	$52
Baltimore	636,251	$32,631,663	$51
Wichita	353,823	$17,879,348	$51
Memphis	671,929	$33,629,566	$50
Fresno	457,719	$21,987,600	$48
Indianapolis	784,242	$37,086,264	$47
Oklahoma City	528,042	$24,958,150	$47
Charlotte/Mecklenburg	771,617	$33,712,263	$44
Philadelphia	1,470,151	$64,096,697	$44
Tulsa	383,764	$15,883,289	$41
Louisville	700,030	$28,412,636	$41
Los Angeles	3,845,541	$144,344,168	$38
Pittsburgh	322,450	$11,969,346	$37
Houston	2,012,626	$70,801,214	$35
Average			**$87**
Median			**$73**

Note 1: Total expenditure includes both operating and capital expenditure, but excludes stadiums, zoos, museums and aquariums.

Note 2: If a city has more than one agency, expenditures are combined.

Note 3: Italic indicates estimate based on prior year information.

waste. As punishment, the company was required to allocate $10 million for the purchase of replacement lands in and around the Bay to be used as parkland. Although events like this are impossible to anticipate, they can still be planned for; planners should always have a wish list of properties to acquire, and mayors should be entrepreneurial enough, in the event of a high-profile corporation trial in the vicinity, to notify the judge that the city would be a candidate for receiving some or all of any legal settlement.

Interagency Transfer

It is often possible to gain parkland through its free transfer from another public agency. Discovery Park, the largest park in Seattle, was acquired free of charge when an old military base was declared surplus by the Pentagon. Flushing Meadow Park in New York—site of two World's Fairs—came into being when the former Corona Dump was transferred from the city's department of sanitation to the department of parks. Atlanta's Freedom Park was created by the transfer of land by the Georgia Department of Transportation when a proposed highway was shelved. And Memphis's Shelby Farm Park was established when an old prison farm was transferred from the Bureau of Prisons to the park department.

Tax-Defaulted Properties

While not free, it is sometimes possible to acquire abandoned property for an inexpensive park (although in most cities this is an arduous process that under current rules may barely be worth the effort). Any property owner who fails to pay his/her land taxes risks having the property confiscated by the government and sold, but an array of legal protections for the owner drags the process out for many years. Chicago has had more success with this than many other places, gaining several hundred acres of parkland thanks to its Tax Reactivation Program, a set of tax-sale procedures that streamline the process. In Cook County (where Chicago is located), if a property is in tax-default, it is put up for purchase through a "scavenger sale." Chicago's Department of Planning and Development can request the county to place a non-cash bid on the land, which covers the cost of all back taxes, penalties, and fees. If no private party outbids the county for the land, the city is given the right to acquire the land, which involves handling all the acquisition legalities (which come to about $2,500 per parcel). In addition to occasional vacant properties sprinkled throughout the city, Chicago used this process to acquire 1,100 abandoned parcels in an ecologically valuable wetland in Calumet on the far south side of the city. (This procedure holds only for vacant land; if a structure is present on the parcel, the process is much more drawn out.)

FINDING AN ALTERNATIVE PUBLIC AGENCY BUYER

In some cases it makes sense for a different public entity—a county, regional, state, or national park agency, or even a port authority, water utility, redevelopment authority, or transportation agency—to create an urban park. This is generally a "Plan B" solution because it introduces different missions and policies into the mix, but it may be preferable to losing the property entirely. Many of these agencies have access to funds, either because their geographies are larger or because they are special-purpose districts with their own taxing authority and revenue stream. Perhaps the most beautiful small park system in New York is made up of the parks of Battery Park City, owned, created, and maintained by a special-purpose redevelopment authority and fully open to the public. Phoenix, Arizona, Duluth, Minnesota, Philadelphia, Pennsylvania, and many other cities have built handsome parks on highway decks over free land made available by transportation departments.

Seattle Parks and Recreation Department

Discovery Park, Seattle's largest park, is on land made available for free when the Pentagon closed a military base at the site. Park planners need to take advantage of such opportunities.

GENERATING MORE REVENUE THROUGH THE BALLOT BOX AND THE LEGISLATURE

Cities generally use one of two means to generate new dedicated revenue for parks creation. One is to secure voter approval of a ballot measure for the purpose. The other is to obligate funds through legislation. The most common ballot mechanisms are general obligation bonds, property taxes, and sales taxes. The most common legislative solutions include impact fees, tax-increment financing, special assessment districts, and business improvement districts.

Voter Approval

General obligation bonds generated by voter approval. Virtually every jurisdiction issues general obligation bonds to pay for high-cost, one-time expenditures (e.g., constructing a road or a public building, buying land, or carrying out a major repair). Bonds are a way to bring in a large amount of money and to repay it gradually and predictably over a long period of time, say, 20 years. The repayment, made on the "full faith and credit" of the

Minnesota Department of Transportation

Some cities, like Duluth, Minnesota, have been able to build parks over highways, on land made available by transportation departments.

jurisdiction, is usually made using money brought in by the property tax or the sales tax. Bonds can be issued based on a vote of the public at large in an election (more common in the western states of the U.S.) or based on a vote of the city or county council (more common in the eastern states of the U.S.). While bonds are used for every imaginable governmental financial need, a percentage of them regularly go for parkland. In the U.S., between 1996 and 2006, according to the Trust for Public Land's "LandVote" database, citizens voted on a total of 1,566 local ballot measures (http://www.tpl.org/tier3_cdl.cfm?content_item_id=12010&folder_id=2386). Of these, 1,206 passed, authorizing the expenditure of $51 billion—more than $18 billion of which went for open space acquisition and parkland creation.

Raising the property tax. Most local jurisdictions have a property tax that pays for a broad base of local services. In a few cases, a small portion of the property tax is permanently earmarked for parkland acquisition (or even parkland maintenance). The benefits of this approach are that it provides a steady source of revenue, is easily administered, distributes the tax burden relatively fairly, and can result in a lot of money from a tiny rate increase. The drawbacks include stiff competition from other interest groups, resistance of lawmakers to earmark funds, and the public's general concern about high property taxes.

Raising the sales tax. Some local jurisdictions have a local sales tax (added on to the state's sales tax). In some cases, that tax is already at its statutory maximum; elsewhere, the state legislature might allow it to be raised minimally (by one-sixteenth or one-eighth of a percent, for instance). Potentially this addition could be earmarked for parks. The benefits are that it can tap into tourism profits generated by park use and amenities, it is relatively easily administered, there are low reporting costs, and it can generate large sums. The drawbacks are that sales taxes are regressive and fall more heavily on the poor (although food and medicine could be exempted to help counter this), and revenues drop when purchasing decreases.

Legislative Measures

General obligation bonds enacted by the legislature. Described above, these bonds can also be authorized by the city or county legislative body, depending on the charter of the jurisdiction.

Instituting an impact fee. Impact fees are common in suburban areas as well as in some cities mostly in the southern and western U.S.; they are less common in the northern and eastern U.S., although some cities have an informal method of getting infrastructure benefits from developers. Among the benefits are the "nexus" between taxing new development and protecting open space—the new parks are required to be located in the general vicinity of the new housing. The drawbacks are that older, park-poor neighborhoods are often not eligible to get impact-fee land if development is miles away. Impact fees can also contribute to higher housing costs. Finally, impact fees are often hard to collect and to bundle so as to actually be able to buy land with them.

Tax Increment Financing. Tax increment financing (TIF) is a municipal revitalization tool whereby a neighborhood receives infrastructure upgrades on the assumption that the resulting increase in property tax revenues due to rising property values brought about by the upgrades (the increment) will generate funds to pay back the initial investment. In other words, neighborhoods that qualify (often an area must be designated as blighted to qualify) are allowed to essentially spend future tax revenue in advance with a promise to repay it. The money is often spent on streetscape improvements or on big-ticket items like convention centers that drive private-sector rehabilitation and renewal. While TIF districts are fairly common, most cities do not use them for parkland acquisition. (Some use them to revitalize neglected parks.) An exception is Chicago, which has spent more than $30 million of TIF money either acquiring parkland or remediating polluted ground for use as parks in degraded or formerly industrial areas. And the whole concept of TIFs and parks may be changing with the newfound realization of the importance of parks as seeds for urban revival. Atlanta is leading the way with the 2006 authorization of a $2 billion Tax Allocation District (a TIF under a different name) for the creation of the Atlanta Beltline, a 22-mile combination greenway park and transit loop around downtown.

Passing a special assessment. Special assessments are gaining in popularity in response to the many limitations placed on property taxes, particularly in California. To many, these assessments seem fairer because they can be more closely linked to the benefits that accrue from the parkland purchased with them. The assessment district's geography can also be pinpointed toward communities that are less tax-averse. This approach has several advantages:

Special assessments are gaining in popularity in response to the many limitations placed on property taxes, particularly in California. To many, these assessments seem fairer because they can be more closely linked to the benefits that accrue from the parkland purchased with them.

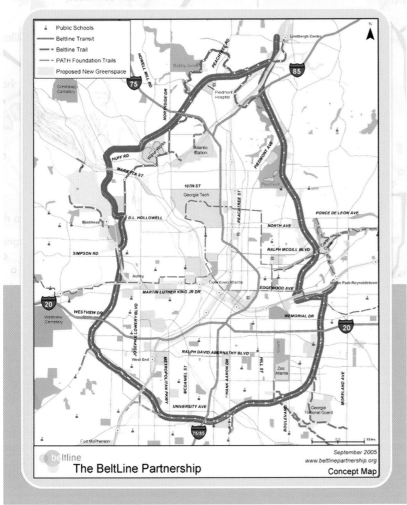

The Beltline Partnership

Atlanta is using a $2 billion Tax Allocation District (a type of Tax Increment Financing tool) to create a 22-mile greenway and transit loop around the city.

- Users finance the acquisition (and even the maintenance) of parkland.
- A predictable revenue stream is generated.
- There is greater accountability in government spending.
- Such assessments can be established in small increments.
- It may be possible to arrange for a tailored election date and election process.

The drawback is that many people oppose them as "a tax by another name."

Creating a business improvement district. A business improvement district (BID) is a special assessment district in a commercial area, usually a downtown. These districts have been extremely successful and popular and are proliferating rapidly, particularly in the eastern U.S. in big cities. Virtually none of them build or rehabilitate parks, however, and only a few even maintain or program parks. (For more on improvement districts, see "Creating a Park Improvement District," below.) The benefits and drawbacks of BIDs are similar to special assessment districts. It's important to recognize, however, that they are only viable in areas sufficiently profitable that owners and renters are willing and able to pay a premium over regular property taxes.

FINDING A PRIVATE PARTNER TO CREATE A PARK

In rare cases, private entities have created parks. Two of the most famous are the Park at Post Office Square in Boston and Yerba Buena Garden in San Francisco. Post Office Square is a unique effort where a consortium of business owners and real estate interests formed a for-profit corporation that constructed an $80 million underground parking garage with a ground-level park. The park is technically owned by the city of Boston but it was fully built (and is fully maintained) through the profits from the garage and a food kiosk concession. Yerba Buena Garden is a $40-million park built in conjunction with the $2 billion mixed-use Yerba Buena redevelopment project in the formerly decrepit Mission District. Technically, the San Francisco Redevelopment Authority is a quasi-public agency, but it operates like a private entity, funding itself through rental payments for its projects.

Thanks to a special law, New York City has a considerable number of privately built vest pocket parks and plazas in the midst of the high-rise canyons of Manhattan. The city's innovative zoning regulation allows developers to gain additional building height in return for reducing the footprint and providing public open space at sidewalk level. (The building owner must also maintain the park.) The most famous of several hundred such microspaces is Paley Park, with its handsome waterfall and wrought-iron chairs.

KEEPING PARKS BEAUTIFUL ONCE THEY HAVE BEEN BUILT

It turns out that keeping a park maintained, properly programmed, and properly used is harder than building one new.

The primary mechanism for sustaining a park system is the municipal park and recreation department. That is its purpose, that is its expertise, and that is what it is there for. Again, research by The Center for City Park Excellence shows that the park agencies whose budgets are above about $85 to $95 per city resident are generally able to maintain their systems to a reasonably high level of quality, cleanliness, safety, and horticultural health.

It turns out that keeping a park maintained, properly programmed, and properly used is harder than building one new.

But many park departments are not funded that well and do not have the money to keep up parks to acceptable standards. Others have one or two parks that represent a special funding challenge because of their size, heavy use, special plantings, historic artifacts, or other factors. In those situations, there are several options to sustain the park, as described in the following paragraphs.

Volunteers

In any metropolitan area, thousands of people are willing and even eager to volunteer in parks. They represent a large, well-motivated, and often highly skilled workforce to help with park cleanup, invasive species removal, simple flower planting, user counting, visitor greeting, assisting with park programs, publicity, office work, and numerous other jobs. The key to a successful program is providing a strong structure within the park department to manage the volunteers, from taking the initial phone call to formally setting times and tasks, to overseeing the work, to ensuring the proper supplies and equipment are available, to handling problems, and even to managing the exit interview or questionnaire.

The city of Seattle, for instance, has a full-time volunteer coordinator and a highly formalized system whereby individuals and organizations even go so far as to sign written contracts specifying what work will be done and what each partner must bring to the table. In many cases, the outcome is an "Adopt-a-Park" contract whereby a local group shows the agency it has the ability to do the volunteer work and agrees to at least a three-year plan of action. In Washington, D.C., the volunteer program of the nonprofit group

Prospect Park Alliance

The key to a successful volunteer program for maintaining parks is good management. Given good management, volunteers, like these people in Prospect Park in Brooklyn, New York, can add significant resources to park development and maintenance.

Washington Parks and People benefits from more than 18,000 hours of donated time per year (time worth about $435,000 on the open market).

It is important to recognize that volunteers are not "free," and that volunteer programs have some of their own complicated dynamics. Of course, volunteers must be treated well and shown they are valued because they are free agents who can easily go to other endeavors if they feel underappreciated. Also, in cities with unionized park workforces, delicate issues often arise related to paid versus unpaid tasks. In general, it must be demonstrated that the work done by volunteers is supplementing rather than replacing that of the paid staff. Lastly, it is important that volunteers be assigned to staff members who are skilled at managing people rather than those who would rather just do the work themselves.

Adopt a Park

This takes the volunteering discussed in the previous section to the next level, arranging for an entity (e.g., a family, an association, a corporation, a school, etc.) to officially take responsibility for a variety of park tasks. The city of San Jose, California, has a robust adopt-a-park/adopt-a-trail program that involves signing a simple contract and agreeing to commit to it for at least one year. More than 200 parks and specific park features (e.g., tennis courts, playgrounds, and walkways) have been adopted by individuals, families, neighborhood associations, high school key clubs, scout troops, Native-American tribes, dog groups, fraternities, religious congregations, and corporations.

A kindred concept is cause-related marketing. Under this scenario a corporation offers to make a small donation to a park agency or friends' group in response to each sale of an item or each use of a service. One of the most successful examples of this approach occurred in the 1980s when the American Express Corporation announced that a small percentage of each transaction would be donated to the National Park Service's effort to rehabilitate the Statue of Liberty.

Nonprofit Organization Contracts

It is possible to pay a nonprofit organization to do the work that volunteers typically do. A preeminent example is found in Philadelphia where Philadelphia Green, a division of the Pennsylvania Horticultural Society, partners with public and private agencies to landscape and maintain public spaces downtown, along city gateway corridors, and in neighborhoods. (See PAS Report No. 506/507 for a fuller discussion of Philadelphia Green's activities.) Philadelphia Green's reputation has risen so high that, in 2003, the Philadelphia Department of Recreation signed a contract turning the maintenance of four of its neighborhood parks over to the nonprofit. That contract was later expanded to nine parks, and then to 50.

Park Conservancies and Maintenance Trust Funds

Following the extraordinary success of the Central Park Conservancy, which raised $300 million between 1980 and 2005 and completely transformed the park, park lovers in many other cities have sought to emulate that model. In most cases, the support organization is designed to rebuild and prop up a single park, such as Prospect Park in Brooklyn, Forest Park in St. Louis, Hermann Park in Houston, and Piedmont Park in Atlanta. In Boston, the Emerald Necklace Conservancy works on the string of seven parks designed by Frederick Law Olmsted. Elsewhere, the Pittsburgh Parks Conservancy and the San Francisco Parks Trust devote their attention to all of their cities' major parks. Most city park conservancies spring up initially as fundraising entities. Typically, they are created by wealthy community leaders who live near a large, signature park that has become run down. Generally, the conservancy works closely with the city department to identify a set of costly needs—often major capital repairs—and then sets out to raise all or a portion of the budgeted amount. Frequently, over time, the experience is so satisfactory that the city gradually turns more and more responsibility to the conservancy, including some of the day-to-day maintenance and operations. In New York, the Central Park Conservancy has become the park's primary manager, with the city covering only 15 percent of the costs and retaining the principal authority to set policy. In the case of Prospect Park, the position of park administrator and Prospect Park Alliance president is held by the same person, who draws a half-paycheck from each of her employers. (This New York City model has not yet been emulated elsewhere as yet.)

Generally, the conservancy works closely with the city department to identify a set of costly needs—often major capital repairs—and then sets out to raise all or a portion of the budgeted amount.

Park Improvement Districts

It is a documented fact that an outstanding park raises the value of surrounding properties (Crompton 2000). This attribute provides an opportunity to use a park as an economic engine—and to use the nearby neighborhood as financial fuel for that engine. Many cities, particularly in the eastern U.S., have passed enabling legislation whereby a self-defined neighborhood can vote to assess itself a fee and then use the funds to make improvements. Generally speaking, passage of the fee requires a majority vote of all the property owners in a specified district; if the vote passes, everyone is assessed, even those who voted against it. Most of these entities are BIDs (see above) that focus on litter clean-up, management of homeless persons, sidewalk washing, and graffiti removal, for example, although a few of them have programs relating to street trees and pocket parks.

New York's Bryant Park Restoration Corporation is fully focused on park improvement and has proved to be an extraordinarily successful undertaking that paid for the $17 million renovation of Bryant Park. It now operates and programs the six-acre parcel. Despite the extra "tax" that nearby storeowners, building operators, and office renters pay to the Restoration Corporation, the growth in activity around the park, resulting in improved business, greater safety, and creation of a distinctive community character, means that virtually everyone in the vicinity believes the effort is worthwhile.

Money-Making Facilities and Programs

In the past, the idea of a "money-making" urban park was anathema, but city budget shortfalls have begun to change some people's thinking. More urban dwellers seem to believe that a clean and beautiful park with some commercial activity is preferable to a dirty, unkempt park entirely free, unbranded, and available to all. Few city parks actually charge an entrance fee, but quite a few parks now have one or more ways of earning money.

The ideal solution is to place the revenue-producing activity underground, out of sight and out of mind. Boston's Post Office Square, San Francisco's Union Square, and Cleveland's Memorial Plaza are all built over money-making parking garages. (Post Office Square advertises itself with: "Park Above, Park Below.") The 45-mile-long W&OD Railroad Trail in Arlington and Fairfax, Virginia, has a lease for an underground fiber-optic line that nets the Northern Virginia Regional Park Authority $375,000 a year.

Prospect Park Alliance

Many cities have groups that have devoted themselves to the preservation of a single park, modeling their programs on the successful Central Park Conservancy. Prospect Park in Brooklyn has its own "Alliance."

Then there are various sports fees. Depending on the culture of the community, there may be more or less willingness to use fees to help defray costs. In virtually all cases, golf fees are well accepted (and some park directors privately refer to golf as a "cash cow"), as are fees for wedding receptions. Almost as accepted are fees for ice skating, roller skating, adult sports leagues, and, sometimes, tennis. Chicago's new Millennium Park includes a "bike station" where commuter and recreational cyclists can store their bikes, take a shower, use clothes lockers, and make use of a bike repair service, all for a fee. And many waterfront parks have marinas and boat slips for lease.

Some park agencies bundle all their revenue-producing divisions into a separate unit, usually known as an "enterprise fund." Enterprise funds operate under different rules than normal public agencies and are expected to cover all their direct and indirect costs. By doing this, agencies can shield

Catering St. Louis

Allowing food concessions that can put revenue in the park budget is an idea whose time has come in the U.S. The Boathouse Restaurant on Post-Dispatch Lake in Forest Park in St. Louis is a money maker and a beauty.

these funds and programs from the normal annual risk of budget cutbacks; the budget deliberations then are conducted solely over the "normal" (non-enterprise) activities of the agency.

A growing source of park revenue stems from the sale of food. Eating in parks has had a long tradition in Europe (and New York's Central Park has had the famous Tavern on the Green since 1934), but most American city park agencies resisted the addition of cafes or dining opportunities until recently. That is now beginning to change, both for financial reasons and because of a new appreciation that a type of urban ambience traverses the formerly bright line between "gritty city" and "pure nature." Pioneer Courthouse Square in Portland, Oregon, now has a Starbucks. Boston's Post Office Square has the Milk Street Café, New York's Madison Square Park has the Union Square Café, and St. Louis's Forest Park has the lively Boathouse restaurant on Post-Dispatch Lake.

Privatizing Concessions

Many park departments undervalue their assets and get a poor return on their concessions. When New York City opened up some of its park programs, services, and amenities to competitive bidding in the early 1980s, it was astounded by the results—the golf program went from a $2 million-a-year money-loser to a $3 million-a-year profit center; the lease on the Wollman Skating Rink brought in $850,000; the tennis center in Forest Hills earned $1.15 million. When the city auctioned off the annual concession for a single hot dog-and-pretzel vendor in Central Park in front of the Metropolitan Museum of Art, the winning bid came in at just under $200,000, making it the most valuable pushcart in the country. All told, between 1979 and 1997,

Central Park Conservancy

the New York Department of Parks and Recreation increased its annual concession and fee income from $2.5 million to an amazing $36 million.

More Maintenance Money through Public Referenda

Although Americans typically vote for billions of dollars of bonds for park and open space acquisition every election cycle, almost no money is ever voted for ongoing park maintenance. Why this is so is not totally clear. Although many states and communities forbid the use of bond money for anything but capital expenditures (i.e., major, one-time items), many have no such provision. It seems to be a cultural phenomenon: people don't want to see bond money sent to the "black hole" of ongoing expenditures. Nevertheless, there are exceptions, and perhaps in the future this cultural bias will change. In Hillsboro, Oregon, voters passed a bond measure that generates $5 million a year in operating funds; 90 percent of the money is earmarked for police and fire protection, but 10 percent is for park operations. In some other localities, even when the overwhelming majority of bond funds must by law go for land acquisition, a 3 percent or 5 percent fraction can be used for operations.

Advertising in Park Facilities

It is nobody's first choice, but more and more cities are accepting advertising and facility naming in return for contributions, gifts, and fees. The new amateur sports stadium on New York's Randalls Island is named after financier Carl Icahn, who gave $10 million. In Chicago's new Millennium Park, it is impossible to avoid the names of corporate donors—from Tribune Rink to Wrigley Square to SBC Plaza to Bank One Promenade to BP Bridge

The lease on the Wollman Skating Rink in New York City's Central Park brought in $850,000 with its lease. Park "owners" often undervalue their assets, and privatization has proved a boon to some.

to Exelon Pavilion. But how else could a city raise $275 million from the private sector for a park?

CONCLUSION

There is no simple solution to the challenge of raising money for park creation and park maintenance, but it can be done, as is clearly shown from the examples I've provided throughout this chapter. The preferred way is to adequately fund the city park and recreation department and let the agency follow its master plan priorities for acquisition and operation. But if the parks and planning communities do not have enough political strength to ensure that outcome, one or more of the alternative approaches I've discussed here become necessary.

CHAPTER 5 REFERENCE

Crompton, John L. 2000. *The Impact of Parks and Open Space on Property Values and the Property Tax Base*. Arlington, Va.: National Recreation and Park Association.

CHAPTER 6

Recommendations for Integrating Park and Open Space Planning in Overall Community Planning

By Megan Lewis, AICP, and Mary Eysenbach

In each chapter of this PAS Report, the author presented suggestions for advancing the practice of parks, recreation, and open space system planning. Chapter 1 discussed what constitutes a park, and placed these spaces within the larger context of a park and open space system in order to release them from certain stereotypes, to elevate their importance, and to help advocates better support them during planning and budgeting, among other goals. Chapter 2 took the idea of elevating their status further and proposed a wide array of park functions and services for both individual parks and the larger systems to better incorporate their value into the community fabric. Chapter 3 provided us with needs assessment process for parks and open space. Chapter 4 presented a survey of recent park system plans in order to better understand the current state of the art and to see if the practice of park planning is moving in the direction that the authors describe in other chapters. And Chapter 5 gave the basics on park funding and creation, noting that obtaining funds for parkland acquisition is often the easier nut to crack; securing funds for ongoing maintenance and support of parks is typically the challenge that communities face.

As a general conclusion to this report, it may be safe to say that parks today are highly valued, deeply loved, and vitally important places within our communities that still need more support. As we have seen a revitalization of cities in the U.S., we have also seen our parks rebound. As community groups take back parks in distressed neighborhoods, residents demand access to green space, and leaders dedicate funds—and political will—to these efforts, we have seen progress all across the country. For this momentum to continue, however, this progress cannot occur piecemeal, and it cannot be left to chance.

How can the ideas presented in this PAS Report be used to support a fundamental shift in park system planning? How can the thoughts and concepts be translated into a mechanism for re-creating park system planning?

In much of our work in APA's research department, we take issues of vital importance to the health of our communities and their residents—physical activity, Brownfields revitalization, hazards mitigation, to name a few—and connect them to the key steps in the planning process, which APA refers to as the "strategic points of intervention." These five points are discussed in the following paragraphs along with our ideas about how the key points of this report about parks can be implemented at each of these stages.

VISIONING AND GOAL SETTING

Visioning identifies and defines issues that a plan will address. During the visioning and goal-setting process, stakeholders identify shared values and develop broad, guiding principles that will guide the plan's contents. Visioning typically includes a discussion of how the community should look in the future, how residents will experience the community, and how proposed changes will affect the quality of life. Within visioning and goal setting, parks and open space goals typically address community appearance, environmental stewardship, and recreation and activity goals of the residents. These visions may extend 20 to 30 years into the future.

As regards parks and open space visioning and goal setting, we recommend the following:

Parks and open space goals typically address community appearance, environmental stewardship, and recreation and activity goals of the residents. These visions may extend 20 to 30 years into the future.

- Create a definition of "parks" and "park system" customized to the particular community's history, assets, and needs.

- Create and confirm a future vision, often with a task force or committee of stakeholders, to create this definition.

- Identify community goals and determine the connection that parks have to achieving those goals.

- Expand the idea of what parks are to ensure that the visioning and goal-setting process asks the right questions of stakeholders—and that the stakeholders involved in the process include these expanded interests, such as public health.

- Develop a framework for the visioning process that reflects this broader definition of parks.

- Focus particular attention on ensuring a balance among the different type of parks available within the system to efficiently achieve the full range of park, recreation, and open space objectives.

- Use a needs assessment process as the basis for determining what your community's park plan should address.

- If using level of service (LOS) standards, customize them for the particular community and make sure they reflect the broad range of functions that parks serve.

- Use anecdotal, qualitative, and quantitative techniques— triangulation — to capture the most accurate picture of the communities needs.

- Undertake a one- to two-year public involvement process (for stand-alone plans) that informs the needs assessment, visioning, and the goals and objectives.

- Create a vision statement to include in plans.

PLANS

Plans are developed to address a wide range of functions and scale, including jurisdictionwide comprehensive plans, subarea plans (neighborhood, downtown, corridor), and functional plans (transit, highway, sewer, water, open space). These plans set the framework for recommended management tools and public investments. Moreover, plans affect public and private sector decisions about where and how development and green areas occur. At the very least, comprehensive plans should contain overarching language regarding how green space is integral to many community goals; the parks and open space functional plan should identify land acquisition priorities and programmatic objectives; and subarea plans should include site-specific improvements.

Our recommendations for addressing parks and open space specifically in the variety of plans that a community creates are contained in the following list.

- Consider how the park system is integrated in the community and how it is linked to the various resources in the community, including the community's natural systems, infrastructure, and land use.

- Incorporate the park system needs and issues into jurisdictionwide comprehensive plans, subarea plans, and functional plans.

- Create a stand-alone park system plan to more specifically address the goals in the other plans. This plan should explicitly describe the relationship between this plan and all other community plans.

- Connect specific community goals to park creation and support (e.g., using parks to revitalize a distressed neighborhood or creating bicycle trails to promote public health or reduce traffic congestion).

- Use the park *system*—not each park—to meet the community needs.

- Develop specific strategies and a detailed plan of action to implement the plan.

- Include an evaluation process.

MANAGEMENT TOOLS

Management tools, which include ordinances, regulations, and incentives, influence where and how things are built. Management tools control the density and layout of the settlement pattern, affect building orientation, and define the amount of green space required based upon adopted plans. Many communities today have an open space dedication ordinance, requiring developers to create public open space within their developments or pay a fee in lieu of a land donation. These ordinances are best used in combination with design guidelines and site design review requirements that complement the parks and open space plan. For instance, instead of simply requiring a certain number of acres from a set of contiguous subdivisions, an informed development review process could create linked open spaces or even one linear park.

Instead of simply requiring a certain number of acres from a set of contiguous subdivisions, an informed development review process could create linked open spaces or even one linear park.

Our recommendations follow.

- Use the regulations, ordinances, and incentives available to planners to implement the park-related goals of the various plans.

- Employ management tools to define the amount of green space required for new developments.

- Use GIS technology to map the park system and to connect the other functions and services of parks to other community resources.

- Create subdivision regulations that identify land to be preserved as open space based on certain qualities and values (e.g., stormwater management, biodiversity, and viewshed protection).

- Use future land-use maps to identify potential linkages between park sites in order to create a network.

- Develop a site plan review process to ensure that new projects follow the goals outlined in the plans and that projects follow both the letter and the spirit of the regulations.

- Use tools (e.g., mandatory dedication ordinances, tax increment finance districts, and business improvement districts) to provide funding for parks.

PUBLIC INVESTMENTS

The capital improvements program (CIP) is the action plan for the plans' objectives. The capital program reflects decision-makers' priorities. In the context of parks, these programs can include improved walking and biking facilities, urban forestry, roof gardens, greenways, sewer and water facilities, and schools. Moreover, planners working in the public sector or as consultants to local governments are well positioned to encourage private-sector investment decisions that affect parks and open space. It is important that parks' improvements be coordinated with other public and private investments to maximize the effectiveness of each. For instance, park improvements designed to help drive community revitalization should be timed to coordinate with other public investments, such as streetscape improvements, as well as private investments, such as new residential or retail developments.

Specifically, we recommend the following actions.

- Continue to support financial measures to acquire parkland, including purchase by the parks department, receiving donated property, finding another public agency to purchase land, or getting more revenue from other sources.

- Pursue ballot measures (typically either bonds or taxes) or legislative solutions to create new financing tools (e.g., impact fees and special assessment districts).

- Differentiate between community needs (of which there are often many) and community priorities (the greatest common needs of the community).

- Keep in mind the widest range of park functions when looking for funding sources.

- Use the five-year CIP as the mechanism to implement plans.

- Use information on the importance and benefits of parks to fund ongoing operations and maintenance.

- Seek creative nonfinancial solutions to keep the parks and the park system attractive and functional (e.g., volunteers, park adoption, contracting with a nonprofit for park management, corporate adoption, and contracting out services).

POLICY

Planners make policy recommendations to planning board officials, elected officials, and other decisions makers. These recommendations may range from the creation of a clean rivers task force to specific implementation policies, such as new land development policies that require developers and new customers to cover the additional cost of extending sewer systems in no growth areas. Planners also help to implement policy. In the case of parks and open space, communities are exploring new policies around issues such as social equity and access to parks; parks and physical activity; urban heat island mitigation; and open space as growth management tools.

By integrating a key community issue into these five strategic points, planners can use the planning process to help ensure parks are discussed when crucial decisions are being made and are considered when key outcomes are being defined.

Our specific recommendations follow.

- Encourage elected officials to be visionaries and support their park systems, from acquisition to maintenance.

- Organize stakeholders from areas related to various park functions (public health, education, and public safety) to become advocates for parks.

Park improvements designed to help drive community revitalization should be timed to coordinate with other public investments, such as streetscape improvements, as well as private investments, such as new residential or retail developments.

- Involve grassroots organizations during the decision-making process to make meaningful policy changes.

- Communicate and promote the importance of parks in all relevant venues so that parks continue to succeed and be relevant.

- Obtain formal adoption of the park plan by city council or appropriate governing body.

Our recommendations for integrating park and open space considerations at these intervention points in the planning process are by no means complete or final. While our principal recommendation is that communities prepare stand-alone parks and open space plans, and integrate them fully with all other community plans, an approach that makes sure that parks and open space are not overlooked for the role they can play in achieving the goals of any plan is critical. While not every community undertakes planning the way we have described it here, identifying possible points of intervention in whatever process the community uses provides opportunities to make improvements at any and every stage of planning. The importance of parks and open space to creating vibrant communities of lasting value has been documented thoroughly throughout the City Parks Forum program. We hope you can use that documentation and your planning process to ensure that the residents of your community have a parks and open space system that is the envy of your neighbors and even the country or world.

Developing a Needs Assessment:
The Oviedo, Florida, Case Study

By David Barth, AICP

Oviedo, located northeast of Orlando in central Florida, is a fast-growing suburban community of approximately 32,000 people. The city's meteoric growth within the past 20 years—from a rural hamlet to a bustling small city—has put a severe strain on its abilities to keep up with residents' increasing parks and recreation needs. In order to develop a "blueprint" for the city's growth and to determine priorities for funding, the city hired the firm of Glatting Jackson Kercher Anglin to prepare a Parks and Recreation Master Plan. The plan was developed from May 2006 to November 2006, and major components included:

1. A Parks and Recreation Needs Assessment to determine top priority needs

2. A long-range Vision for the build-out of the community

3. An Implementation Strategy to build the top priority improvements.

The following techniques were used in the Needs Assessment phase of the project to determine community priorities (see Chapter 3 of the PAS Report for a further explanation of each of these techniques):

1. *Anecdotal Techniques*
   - Population/Demographic Analysis
   - Site Visits and Existing Conditions Analysis

2. *Qualitative Techniques*
   - Interviews with city Council members
   - Steering Committee Workshop
   - Parks and Recreation Staff Workshop
   - Stakeholder/Focus Group Meetings
   - Public Workshop

3. *Quantitative Techniques*
   - Level of Service (LOS) Analysis—Facilities
   - Level of Service (LOS) Analysis—Acreage
   - Level of Service (LOS) Analysis—Service Areas
   - Telephone Survey

The following sections summarize our findings.

POPULATION/DEMOGRAPHIC ANALYSIS

Glatting Jackson evaluated available census data to identify population trends and inferred recreation needs. Table A-1 reflects Census statistics showing the changes in the city from 1980 to 2000 in terms of total population, age, race, and poverty:

The statistics show how Oviedo has grown by leaps and bounds in recent decades. Between 1980 and 1990, the total population more than tripled; between 1990 and 2000, it more than doubled to reach 26,316. The city is primarily white, but with a growing Hispanic population. Census statistics also show the variability in age groups over the decades: from 1980 to 2000, the percentage of the population over 60 has declined sharply, whereas the percentage of those under age 20 has remained similar despite a spike in the 1990 Census of children younger than 10. Compared to the rest of Florida, Oviedo differs in that its population has a significantly higher median income and a lower percentage of people older than 60.

TABLE A-1. OVIEDO, FLORIDA, GROWTH ACCORDING TO CENSUS STATISTICS, 1980–2000

	1980	1990	2000	FLORIDA 2000
Total Population	3,074	11,114	26,316	15,982,378
Race: % White	69.62%	84.18%	83.50%	78.00%
Race: % Black	29.47%	12.24%	8.80%	14.60%
Race: % Asian	no data	1.59%	2.40%	1.70%
Race: % Hispanic Origin	1.40%	6.91%	12.20%	16.80%
Race: % Other	no data	1.84%	3.60%	3.00%
Age: Under 10	17.01%	23.10%	17.80%	12.40%
Age: 11–19	18.25%	9.20%	16.20%	12.90%
Age: 20–34	23.19%	32.60%	20.00%	18.80%
Age: 35–59	27.46%	27.70%	37.70%	33.50%
Age: 60+	14.09%	7.40%	8.00%	22.20%
Median Income	$15,188	no data	$64,119	$45,625
% under Poverty Line	13.70%	no data	4.60%	12.50%

*Because Oviedo did not experience major growth until the 1970s, little Census data is available prior to 1980.
Source: U.S. Census Bureau

Findings

The growing youth population, combined with the growing Hispanic population, *may* indicate the need for more athletic fields and sports programs, particularly youth and adult soccer. The higher median income and lower percentage of people older than 60 *may* indicate the need for more facilities and programs for active adults, such as bike paths, tennis courts, and performing arts/cultural facilities.

SITE VISITS AND EXISTING CONDITIONS ANALYSIS

In May, 2006, Glatting Jackson visited the city's major parks and facilities; in addition to recording site observations, the seven properties were all systematically evaluated on three different components:

FIGURE A-1. EXISTING PARK LOCATIONS, OVIEDO FLORIDA, 2006

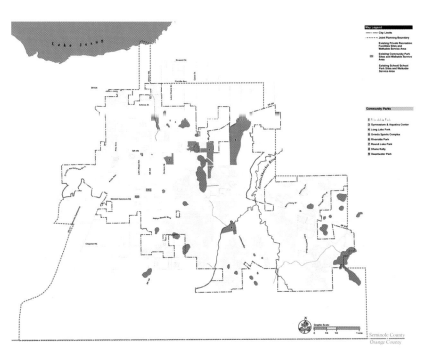

Source: Glatting Jackson Kercher Anglin

1. Proximity, access, and linkages

2. Opportunities

3. Physical conditions

The park system currently consists of six community parks and three special use facilities, including the recent addition of the new gymnasium and aquatic facility. Generally, parks are well-maintained with the gymnasium and aquatic facility exhibiting an especially high standard. Many of the parks, however, lack shaded areas and experience problems with irrigation. There is also a need to upgrade minor amenities, such as signage and trashcans. The parks are predominantly programmed in their uses and are well used: in a previous survey, 78 percent of Oviedo respondents reported they had visited a community park within the past year.

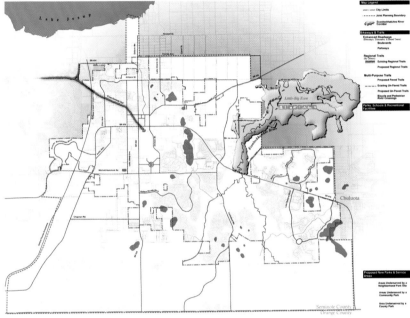

FIGURE A-2. EXISTING TRAIL LOCATIONS, OVIEDO, FLORIDA, 2006

Source: Glatting Jackson Kercher Anglin

In addition to parks, there are the beginnings of a multipurpose trail network in and around Oviedo.

Seminole County has planned and partially built the Cross-Seminole County Trail, which connects Oviedo to Winter Garden via a paved recreational trail. When it is complete, the trail will travel more than 24 miles through the county. Currently, there is a major trailhead in the heart of Oviedo, with another proposed trail traveling southwest towards Winter Park. Portions of the trail double as the path of the Florida National Scenic Trail, which blazes 33 miles through the county and traverses northern edge of Oviedo.

Figure A-3 on the following page compares the seven parks' performances in terms of the three evaluation areas.

Findings

Overall, the city's parks are in good condition. There are multiple opportunities for partnerships and revenue generation from many of the parks, and all parks have adequate street access, emergency vehicle access, and evidence of maintenance standards. Areas that need the most improvement are park aesthetics, programming flexibility, and grounds conditions. Although most of the parks perform rather well across the criteria, Sweetwater Park and Round Lake Park are lagging behind the others.

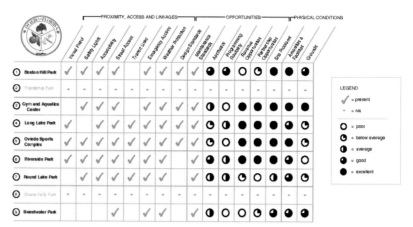

FIGURE A-3. CHART OF PARK OVERALL CONDITIONS, OVIEDO, FLORIDA, 2006 (BASED ON ON-SITE EVALUATIONS)

Source: Glatting Jackson Kercher Anglin

INTERVIEWS WITH CITY COUNCIL MEMBERS

Glatting Jackson conducted interviews with four member of city council and the mayor between June 21 and 22, 2006. Following are the key questions asked during each interview, as well as a summary of the responses.

Question 1: We think of the ideal parks system as having all of the following components (as shown on the attached model):

- Urban Parks and Civic Gathering Spaces
- Small Neighborhood Green Spaces
- Small Neighborhood Parks
- Large Community Parks
- Large Regional Parks
- Community Centers
- Cultural and Historical Facilities
- Special Use Facilities
- Beach/Water Access
- Greenways, Bikeways and Trails
- Public Transit
- Shaded Streets, Avenues, and Parkways w/Sidewalks

   Is this consistent with your own ideas?

Response: All four members of Council and the Mayor agreed that ideal parks systems have all of the above components.

Question 2: Attached is a survey that we use to determine community needs and priorities. Of the facilities listed, which do you believe are needed most in your community?

Response (numbers in parentheses note that the number of times the same comment was recorded):

- More football/multi-purpose fields (planned fields at Shane Kelly may suffice) (4)
- Need more fishing piers: Long Lake, Round Lake, Econ, Long Lake (3)
- Need to fix up existing properties, many are underused and/or in disrepair (e.g., Riverside Recreation Center interior, Round Lake, Boston Hill) (3)
- More baseball fields (especially because Kings Street Little League is losing fields at Methodist Church) (3)
- Don't need any more baseball fields (2)

- Improve bicycle trails, sidewalks, trails in conjunction w/city streets (2)
- Dog parks (2); possibly in conjunction with Winter Springs
- Basketball courts (2)
- Tennis courts (2)
- Need more picnic areas (2) (not secluded)
- Multipurpose indoor/outdoor performance/recreation/civic center, library, museum (2) (Blake Library, for example)
- Museum in the downtown (part of civic center) (2)
- Need public boat ramp on Long Lake (1)
- Roller Hockey rink would be nice; multifunction (1)
- Enhanced security (1)
- Like facilities that make Oviedo unique, including equestrian facility (1)
- Not sure that vast majority of residents know about available parks, (e.g. stage at Riverside Park), especially passive facilities (1)
- Need a marketing plan (1)
- Need to improve fields at OSC (1)
- Need more jogging/hiking trails (1)
- Need more multipurpose fields (1)
- Equestrian facility is needed (1)
- Maintaining Twin Rivers as a golf course (1)
- Covered playgrounds (1)
- Enlarge Riverside pool (1)
- Playgrounds/tot lots (1)
- Canoe/kayak access (1)
- Partner with churches, YMCA, especially for at-risk programs (1)
- No parks on northwestern border

Question 3: Typically we find that most communities need millions of dollars to meet both current and future parks, recreation, open space, and cultural needs. Significant funding sources are shown on the following chart. Which of these would you support?

Response (numbers in parentheses note that the number of times the same comment was recorded and comments):

- Bond referendum (5)
- Slightly raise property taxes (for specific projects) (2)
- Need to promote referendum under "Master Parks and Recreation Plan"(1)
- Corporate sponsorship/naming rights (1)
- Citizens expect a certain level of service for their property taxes (1)
- In favor of borrowing money, paying it back (1)
- Phase 1 of $10 million may be reasonable to bond; taxes, franchise fees, etc. being scrutinized; leverage with grants and other funding sources(1)

Question 4: Most communities can't do everything themselves; what partnerships do you think would be most beneficial to pursue?

Response (numbers in parentheses note that the number of times the same comment was recorded):

- University of Central Florida (2)
- Schools (1)
- County (1)

- State (1)
- Closer relationship with organized groups (1); need to find out what they can contribute (beyond baseline)
- Do it on our own (1)
- Need to branch out, get sponsorships—Oviedo is a reputable city (1)

General Comments

- Like the parks the way they are
- Need to have an annual Repair and Replacement Program
- Need to fix up Round Lake, Sweetwater Parks, Boston Hill, other parks
- Equestrian center is being built at Shane Kelley, whether needed or not
- Must communicate well with citizens
- Very few recreation facilities generate revenues; equestrian is an exception because it covers operational costs and also brings revenues into the area
- Concerns over increase in PWC use on Long Lake
- City considering making a charter change to allow use of revenue bonds without citizen approval
- Need to expand number of respondents
- Need to compare phone list to registered voters, increase to 300+
- City of "kids and cul-de-sacs"
- Need to upgrade, complete what we have before we build new projects

Findings

All four council members and the mayor agreed that an ideal parks system includes each of the components outlined above, while top priorities (those mentioned by 50 percent or more for the city currently include:

- More football/multi-purpose fields (planned fields at Shane Kelly may suffice) (4)
- Need more fishing piers (3)
- Need to fix up existing properties, many are underutilized and/or in disrepair (e.g. Riverside Recreation Center interior, Round Lake, Boston Hill) (3)
- More baseball fields (especially because Kings Street Little League is losing fields at Methodist Church) (3)

The fundraising method preferred by all five respondents was the bond referendum; multiple organizations and agencies were mentioned as important partnership opportunities, but only the University of Central Florida was mentioned by more than one person.

STEERING COMMITTEE WORKSHOP

Glatting Jackson facilitated a workshop with the city's Steering Committee on June 20, 2006. General comments from the committee included:

- "Need more soccer fields"
- "The facilities we have are great. We need more diversification, more open space, covered walking, hiking, biking areas. Areas to sit and enjoy. Gathering places! No more ball fields!"
- "[Parks] not available to the public, just leagues"
- "Need to improve appearance of parks"
- "Not enough multi-purpose fields"
- "Staffing and maintenance need to catch up with capital improvements"
- "All the parks should be interconnected by pedestrian, bike trails"

- More cultural activities are needed.

- Sidewalks/connections between neighborhoods.

- Pedestrian connections.

- "The connection areas between the new and old downtown should be made accessible linking the city from north to south."

Committee members were asked to complete the needs assessment survey being used for the telephone survey. Nine members participated in the survey. The following are the most common responses regarding the need for more facilities:

- Covered Playgrounds (9)

- General Multi-purpose Fields (8)

- Football/Soccer/Rugby fields (7)

- Paved Bicycle Riding/Skating Trails (7)

- Playgrounds or Tot Lots (7)

- Dog Parks (6)

- Performance Center/Auditorium (5)

- Special Events Area/Outdoor Amphitheater (5)

- Youth/Teen Centers (5)

- Canoeing or Kayaking Launches (5)

- Basketball Courts (5)

- Physical Fitness Trails (5)

Findings

Many Steering Committee members (7) only rated park maintenance as "satisfactory" and recreational activities as "satisfactory." Top priority needs:

- Covered Playgrounds

- General "multi-purpose" fields

- Paved Bicycle-Riding/Skating trails

- Playgrounds or Tot-Lots

PARKS AND RECREATION STAFF WORKSHOP

Glatting Jackson conducted one workshop with the city of Oviedo Parks and Recreation staff on June 20, 2006. General comments about park resources included:

- "The upkeep of these parks needs a lot of work"; "signage"

- "They need maintenance"

- "Offers a variety of programs; could use additional funding"

- "The [parks] are fantastic!"

- "Good variety of programs—need to get word out to all residents as to what is offered"

City Parks and Recreation staff members were also asked to complete the telephone survey. Seven (7) staff members completed the survey; the following were the most common responses to facilities the city of Oviedo needs more of:

- Covered playgrounds (7)

- Special events area/outdoor amphitheater (7)

- Dog parks (7)

- Cultural centers/museums (6)

- Football/soccer/rugby fields (6)

- Sidewalks (6)

- Fishing piers (6)
- Paved bicycle riding/skating trails (5)
- Performance center/auditorium (5)
- Gymnasiums (5)
- Playgrounds or tot lots (5)
- Baseball/softball fields (5)
- Youth/teen centers
- Volleyball courts (5)
- General multipurpose fields (4)
- Golf courses (4)
- Senior citizen center (4)
- Physical fitness trails (4)
- Camping sites (4)
- Canoeing/kayaking launches (4)

Findings

Parks and recreation staff members unanimously agreed that the city needs more covered playgrounds, dog parks, and special events areas/outdoor amphitheaters. Six staff members also noted rugby/football fields, sidewalks, and cultural centers/ museums as needs. Most also felt that park maintenance needs to be improved.

FOCUS GROUP MEETINGS

Glatting Jackson conducted a focus group workshop on June 21, 2006, including the following groups:

- Central Florida United Soccer Club
- City of Oviedo
- Friends of Winter Miles
- Girls & Boys Town
- Hagerty High School
- OHS and Pop Warner
- Oviedo Babe Ruth Baseball/Softball
- Oviedo Horseshoe Club
- Oviedo Police Department
- Oviedo YMCA

A total of 15 participants attended the meetings. All participants were asked the following:

Question 1: What parks and recreation needs (facilities, programs, operation, maintenance, etc) does your group have?

Question 2: Of these needs, what are your top three priorities?

Question 3: How can your group help the city meet these needs?

The following is a summary of each group's recreational needs and priorities.

Oviedo Babe Ruth Baseball/Softball:

Needs:

- Fix Musco lighting on all fields
- Scoreboard lights or new scoreboards
- Concessions
- Fields cut to level conditions
- More fields so Oviedo Babe Ruth is not having 2-3 teams per practice slots

- Working Clean Restrooms on softball side of complex
- Host state and regional tournaments
- Electricity to batting cages

Priorities:

- Scoreboard lights or new scoreboards
- Concessions
- More fields

Oviedo YMCA

Needs:

- Soccer field with lights
- Football field
- Baseball fields
- Basketball gym

Priorities:

- Soccer fields with lights
- Football fields
- Basketball gym

Girls and Boys Town of Central Florida

Needs:

- Large play area for younger kids
- Nature trails
- Community center for kids to play in/host shows, arts, events
- More large pavilion areas for parties/events

Priorities:

- Large play area for younger age kids
- Nature trails
- Community center for kids to play in/host shows, arts, events
- More large pavilion areas for parties/events

Hagerty High School – Pop Warner

Needs:

- Swimming facility (Olympic-sized)
- Pop Warner dedicated football fields
- Practice facility for cheer and football
- Off-season leagues
- Open-field facility

Priorities:

- Football Fields
- Cheer facility with mat storage

Friends of Winter Miles (Equestrian Group)

Needs:

- Horse park: show ring/arena, equipment shed, barn/stable

Priorities:

- Show ring/arena
- Equipment shed

- Barn/Stable

City of Oviedo Development Services

Needs:

- Teen and senior centers
- Soccer fields
- Volleyball courts
- Connected trail system
- First Night New Years Eve celebration
- Open play fields (greens)

Priorities:

- Teen/senior community center
- Soccer fields and volleyball courts
- First night celebration
- Open play fields and trail system

Oviedo Horseshoe Club

Needs:

- Expand parking area
- Improve bathroom facilities
- Replace trees uprooted by hurricanes
- Lift restrictions on court lighting
- Provide a secure bulletin board
- Install facility to clean horseshoes
- Provide signs for building and entrance to park

Priorities:

- Expand parking area
- Improve bathroom facilities
- Replace trees uprooted by hurricanes

Central Florida United Soccer Club

Needs:

- One multipurpose field
- Three lighted soccer fields
- Additional fields (2 to 4 fields)
- PAC push band issues
- Push for special assessments to property taxes

Priorities:

- One multi-purpose field
- Additional fields
- PAC push bond issues

Findings

Focus group members mostly noted different needs from one another, but more than one organization mentioned a need for soccer fields, open field facilities, lighting for sports fields, an expanded trails system, and a community center. The only consistent facility mentioned as a priority was open field facilities.

PUBLIC WORKSHOP

The city hosted a public workshop on July 26, 2006, but no community members attended. Based on the consistent findings from the other Needs Assessment techniques, the city and consultants decided that it was not necessary to reschedule the workshop.

LEVEL OF SERVICE (LOS) ANALYSIS—ACREAGE

The Oviedo Comprehensive Plan (Recreation and Open Space Element) establishes a minimum Level of Service (LOS) standard of:

- 2 acres of Neighborhood Park/1,000 population
- 2 acres of Community Park/1,000 population
- 25 percent of developable acreage as open space

[Please note that regional-level parks have LOS standards set by Seminole County.]

Based on these standards, Oviedo is deficient in neighborhood parks by 63 acres, but has a surplus of community park area by 95 acres. If the city maintains current levels of acreage, the deficiency in neighborhood parks will increase to 77 acres by the year 2010 based on population projections; conversely, the city will continue to have a large surplus of community park acreage. Figures A-4 and A-5 detail this analysis:

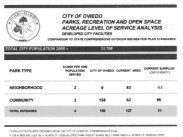

Source: City of Oviedo, Florida

FIGURE A-4. LEVEL OF SERVICE ANALYSIS FOR PARKS, OVIEDO, FLORIDA, 2005

Source: City of Oviedo, Florida

FIGURE A-5. LEVEL OF SERVICE ANALYSIS FOR PARKS, OVIEDO, FLORIDA, POPULATION PROJECTION FOR 2010

An interesting aspect of Oviedo's Comprehensive Plan is that it designates that "the development, operation, and maintenance of [neighborhood] parks shall be a neighborhood responsibility," with no general city funding. The direct result of this policy is a deficiency of neighborhood parks. Even when taking the private facilities into account, Oviedo still has a deficiency of 15 acres of neighborhood parks, and the deficiency will only worsen as the population grows. (See Figures A-6 and A-7.)

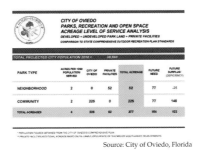

Source: City of Oviedo, Florida

FIGURE A-6. LEVEL OF SERVICE ANALYSIS FOR PARKS, BOTH PUBLIC AND PRIVATE FACILITIES, OVIEDO, FLORIDA, 2005

Source: City of Oviedo, Florida

FIGURE A-7. LEVEL OF SERVICE ANALYSIS FOR PARKS, BOTH PUBLIC AND PRIVATE FACILITIES, OVIEDO, FLORIDA, POPULATION PROJECTION FOR 2010

Findings

While flush with community park acreage, the city is deficient in neighborhood parks. If trends and policy remains the same in designating neighborhood parks as a private responsibility, there will be a deficiency of 25 acres of neighborhood parks to meet the Comprehensive Plan's Level of Service by the year 2010.

LEVEL OF SERVICE (LOS) ANALYSIS—FACILITIES

Florida's SCORP also contains facility standards showing the number of residents served by various types of recreation facilities, e.g. 1 tennis court/2,000 residents, based on surveys of other communities around the State. Oviedo has adopted these facility standards as follows:

- Tennis: 1 court/1,000 population, or 1 lighted court/5,000 population
- Basketball: 1 court/5,000 population
- Baseball/Softball fields: 1 field/2,000 population or 1 lighted field/5,000 population

Figure A-8 shows that, according to the SCORP standards, the city is currently "deficient" in almost all types of facilities. If not addressed, this deficiency will worsen by 2010 as is also shown in Figure A-8.

CITY OF OVIEDO
PARKS, RECREATION AND OPEN SPACE
FACILITY LEVEL OF SERVICE ANALYSIS
COMPARISON TO STATE COMPREHENSIVE OUTDOOR RECREATION PLAN STANDARDS

| TOTAL CITY POPULATION 2005 = | 31,760 | | | | | | | | |

| TOTAL PROJECTED CITY POPULATION 2010 = | 38,590 | | | | | | | | |

ACTIVITY	POPULATION SERVED	CITY OF OVIEDO	SCHOOL/ COUNTY	PRIVATE FACILITIES	TOTAL	CURRENT NEED	CURRENT SURPLUS/ (DEFICIENCY)	FUTURE NEED	FUTURE SURPLUS/ (DEFICIENCY)
BICYCLING (MILES)	5,000	0	1.5	0	2	6	-5	8	-6
CAMPING (ACRES)	6,750	0	0	0	0	5	-5	6	-6
BOAT RAMPS (LANES)	5,000	0	0	2	2	6	-4	8	-6
FISHING (800' OF PIER)	5,600	0	0	0	0	6	-6	7	-7
HIKING (MILES)	6,750	0	1.5	0	2	5	-3	6	-4
HORSEBACK RIDING (MILES)	5,000	0	0	0	0	6	-6	8	-8
PICNICKING	6,000	54	0	0	54	5	49	6	48
BASEBALL/SOFTBALL	5,000	12	9	0	21	6	15	8	13
BASKETBALL	5,000	6.5	6	7	20	5	14	8	12
FOOTBALL/SOCCER/RUGBY	6,000	3	2	0	5	5	0	6	-1
MULTI-PURPOSE FIELD	10,000	2	5	3	10	3	7	4	6
GOLF (18 HOLES)	50,000	0	0	1	1	1	0	1	0
RACQUETBALL/HANDBALL	10,000	3	13	1	17	3	14	4	13
SHUFFLEBOARD	6,000	0	0	10	10	5	5	6	4
SWIMMING POOL	25,000	2	0	7	9	1	8	2	7
TENNIS	2,000	6	12	23	41	16	25	19	22
VOLLEYBALL	6,000	0	0	0	0	5	-5	6	-6

* POPULATION FIGURES OBTAINED FROM THE CITY OF OVIEDO COMPREHENSIVE PLAN
CROSS SEMINOLE TRAIL
WILDERNESS TRAIL ALONG ECONLOCKATCHEE RIVER THAT IS PART OF THE LITTLE BIG ECON FOREST
WHILE THESE POOLS DO NOT MEET SCORP STANDARDS (4,300 sq.ft), THEY ARE FULLFILLING A NEED AT A NEIGHBORHOOD LEVEL

Source: City of Oviedo, Florida

FIGURE A-8. FACILITY LEVEL OF SERVICE ANALYSIS, OVIEDO, FLORIDA, 2005, AND POPULATION PROJECTION FOR 2010

Findings

The city is deficient in almost all types of recreational facilities except for picnicking, baseball/softball fields.

SERVICE AREA ANALYSIS

The Service Area Analysis is one of the most useful quantitative tools for assessing parks and recreation needs. The purpose of the analysis is to determine how far residents must walk, bike or drive to get to a park. The Service Area Analysis for Oviedo assumes a desirable walking distance of one-half mile ("service area") for every resident to get to a Neighborhood Park, and a two-mile service area for every resident to access a larger Community Park. These service areas are consistent with the classifications established in NRPA's *Park, Recreation, Open Space and Greenway*

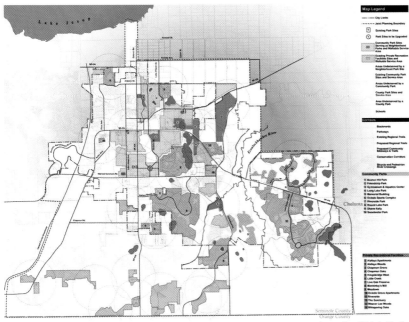

FIGURE A-9. NEIGHBORHOOD PARKS WITHIN ONE-HALF-MILE WALKING RADIUS OF OVIEDO, FLORIDA, RESIDENTS, 2005

Source: City of Oviedo, Florida

Guidelines; the one-half-mile service area is also consistent with the Oviedo Comprehensive Plan Recreation and Open Space Element.

Figure A-9 shows that many Oviedo residents do not have access to a neighborhood park within one-half mile walk of their homes. Even if the city's community parks are counted as neighborhood parks, many residents still live outside a one-half-mile radius.

Figure A-10 shows that more residents have access to a Community Park within a two-mile drive or bike ride from their homes, but those residents are also in the northern and central areas of town. Again, residents in the newer sections of the city, especially in the southeast quadrant, currently have no community park facilities despite the city's surplus acreage.

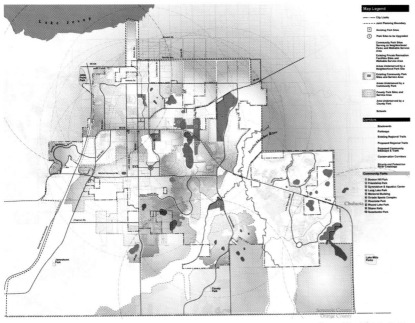

FIGURE A-10. COMMUNITY PARKS WITHIN TWO-MILE DRIVING RADIUS OF OVIEDO, FLORIDA, RESIDENTS, 2005

Source: City of Oviedo, Florida

Findings

Consistent with the LOS Analysis for park land and facilities, there is a great deficiency in neighborhood parks. What the LOS analysis did not show was the great distribution imbalance of community park acreage. Those citizens in the central and northern parts of Oviedo are served quite well by the existing system, whereas those on the southwest do not have any community park access within two miles of their homes.

TELEPHONE SURVEY

Haysmar, Inc, a Research and Analysis firm hired by Glatting Jackson, conducted a telephone survey of city residents to determine their attitudes and opinions regarding the city's Parks and Recreation System.

The survey reached 400 respondents with a population distribution similar to that identified by the 2000 Census. Oviedo responses show an active younger community than many in Florida, with bicycle riding and swimming reported at higher rates and boating, golf, and non-participation at lower rates than in similar communities.

When asked what the city needs more of (in terms of park resources), the most common responses (responses by more than 60 percent of those surveyed) were:

- Outdoor/special events amphitheaters
- Cultural centers/museums
- Performance centers/auditoriums
- Youth/teen centers.

Those park resources mentioned by over 50 percent of those surveyed include covered playgrounds, senior citizen centers, fishing piers, and dog parks.

For funding, 50 percent of respondents reported that they would be unwilling to pay increased property taxes, but 56.5 percent would support increased user fees for facilities. Survey respondents overwhelmingly (72.5 percent) do not support the use of city funds to develop equestrian facilities at Shane Kelley Park.

Overall, the survey shows the residents are generally satisfied with the parks system: 61.5 percent rate maintenance as satisfactory and 66 percent rate programs as satisfactory.

Findings

Residents are generally satisfied with the existing parks system, but note the following needs:

- Need outdoor special events/amphitheater (63.9 percent)
- Cultural centers/museums (61.9 percent)
- Performance centers/auditoriums (60.0 percent)
- Youth/teen centers (60.4 percent)
- Covered playgrounds (58.9 percent)
- Senior citizens center (54.9 percent)
- Fishing piers (51.6 percent)
- Dog parks (50.1 percent)
- Canoeing or kayaking (49.6 percent)
- Hiking/nature trails—unpaved (49.4 percent)
- Sidewalks (49.4 percent)
- Bicycle/skating trails—paved (49.1 percent)

SUMMARY OF NEEDS

Figure A-11 summarizes the results from each of the Needs Assessment techniques. A "city seal" symbol indicates that over 50 percent of respondents participating in the technique feel that that the facility is a priority need. The "Telephone Survey percent" column indicates the percentage of survey respondents who stated that the city "needs more" of the facility.

Based on the various Needs Assessment techniques, top priority needs for the city of Oviedo include:

- Outdoor special events/amphitheater
- Cultural centers/museums
- Performance center/auditorium
- Youth/teen centers
- Covered playgrounds
- Fishing piers
- Dog parks

These needs are consistent with an urbanizing community; in essence the city is transitioning from a bedroom community to a "real" city, and residents are requesting the types of civic, social and meeting facilities associated with traditional municipalities.

Other needs include:

- Bicycle/skating trails—paved
- General "multipurpose" play fields
- Physical fitness trails/jogging and hiking trails—paved
- Football/soccer/rugby fields
- Upgrade existing facilities

The results of the Needs Assessment were incorporated into the citywide Vision Plan, and also formed the basis for the first-phase (10-year) Capital Improvements Program.

FIGURE A-11. SUMMARY OF NEEDS ASSESSMENT

Needs/Priorities Summary	Telephone Survey %	Telephone Survey	Interview with Council + Mayor	Steering Committee Workshop	Parks and Recreation Staff Workshop	Focus Group Meetings	Level of Service	Existing Conditions Analyses
Outdoor Special Events/Amphitheater	63.9%	●		●	●			
Cultural Centers/Museums	61.9%	●			●	●		
Performance Center/Auditorium	60.9%	●		●	●			
Youth/Teen Centers	60.4%	●		●	●	●		
Covered Playgrounds	58.9%	●		●	●			●
Senior Citizens Center	54.9%	●			●	●		
Fishing Piers	51.6%	●	●		●		●	
Dog Parks	50.1%	●	●	●	●			
Canoeing and Kayaking, Boat Ramps	49.6%			●	●		●	
Hiking/Nature Trails - Unpaved	49.4%					●	●	
Sidewalks	49.4%			●	●			●
Bicycle/Skating Trails - Paved	49.1%			●	●	●		
General "Multi-Purpose" Play Fields	47.4%		●	●	●	●		
Physical Fitness Trails/Jogging and Hiking Trails — Paved	43.9%			●	●	●	●	
Playgrounds or Tot Lots	42.4%			●	●			
Football/Soccer/Rugby Fields	39.8%		●	●	●	●		
Basketball Courts	31.6%			●		●		
Baseball/Softball Fields	23.3%		●	●		●		
Horse Back Riding Trails	31.1%						●	
Upgrade Existing Facilities			●		●	●		●

Source: Glatting Jackson Kercher Anglin

Park Plans Matrices

1. Table B-1. General Elements 112

2. Table B-2. Programmatic Elements...114

3. Table B-3. Implementation Elements 118

TABLE B-1. GENERAL ELEMENTS

PLAN JURISDICTION	ALEXANDRIA, VA	BELLEVUE, WA	DENVER, CO	EUGENE, OR
TITLE	Alexandria Open Space Plan	Parks and Open Space System Plan	Game Plan: Creating a Strategy for our Future	Parks, Recreation and Open Space (PROS) Comprehensive Plan
PUBLISH DATE	2002	September 2003	April 2003	2003
TIME FRAME (YEARS)	Not mentioned	17 years (until 2020)	50 years	5 to 10 years
PLAN AREA (PHYSICAL BOUNDARIES)	City of Alexandria	City of Bellevue	City and County of Denver	City of Eugene and area outside city but within urban growth boundary. Includes some recommendations for areas outside UGB.
PLANNING SUB-AREAS	3 planning areas	14 subareas	80 neighborhoods	6 subareas
PARK SYSTEM AND DEFINITION	System defined by 5 layers: Primary uses (active, passive, trails, and streetscape/scenic roadways), secondary characteristics (specific uses and character of space), service area (users, geographic), ownership, and maintenance	Defined in terms of the standards: mini-park, neighborhood park, community park, waterfront access, and natural areas/wildlife corridors/greenways. Recreation facilities defined separately: trail systems, community recreation centers, and athletic facilities.	Plan uses "City in a Park" concept, which allows for expanded park definition to include green infrastructure, tree canopy, environmental benefits, recreation as "re-creation," "green streets," schoolyards, "breathing spaces," and rooftops.	Classification system based on park types: neighborhood park, community park, urban plaza, metro park, natural area park, linear park/greenway, and special use facility.
GRAPHS	No	Yes, population and funding	Yes, funding	Yes, planning process, plan development, population, and plan framework
MAPS	Yes, several	Yes, several	Yes, several	Yes, 1 map of existing and needed parks, open space, and recreation resources
TABLES	One: Open Space Comparison between Select American Cities	Yes, in the subarea inventory and analysis section	Yes, funding	Yes, proposed park standard, financing options, and inventory by subarea. Several in Project and Priority Plan
APPENDICES	Yes, open space classification overview, summary of planning district meetings, and summary of open space summit concerns	None noted	6 appendices: glossary, goals and objectives, learning landscapes, green streets, water conservation plan, and references	2 appendices: park classifications and existing resources. Also includes a bibliography
OFFICIALLY ADOPTED?	Not noted in the plan.	Yes, officially adopted by Bellevue City Council September 2003	Not noted in the plan.	Not noted in the plan.
WEB ADDRESS	http://alexandriava.gov/recreation/general/OpenSpacehome.html	www.ci.bellevue.wa.us/page.asp?view=21418	www.denvergov.org/dephome.asp?depid=1111	http://www.eugene-or.gov/portal server.pt?space=Community Page&cached=true&parentname =CommunityPage&parentid =0&in_hi_userid=2&control =SetCommunity&CommunityID =217&PageID=1360

INDIANAPOLIS-MARION COUNTY, IN	NASHVILLE, TN	PORTLAND, OR	SEATTLE, WA	VIRGINIA BEACH, VA
Park, Recreation, and Open Space Plan	Metropolitan Parks and Greenways Master Plan	Parks 2020 Vision	Parks and Recreation Plan 2000	Virginia Beach Outdoors Plan 2000
2004	2002	2001	2000	2000
5	20	20	20 years (6 years on action items)	5 to 10 years
Marion County (excluding 4 jurisdictions)	Nashville and Davidson County	City of Portland	City of Seattle	City of Virginia Beach
By township	14 planning areas	6 subareas	Into 4 sectors	By 3 geographic areas and within them 9 planning areas
New classification from 2000 plan: regional parks, community parks, neighborhood parks, mini parks, special use parks (various), golf courses, natural resource areas, sports complexes, monuments/memorials, greenways, family recreation centers, aquatic centers, and environmental education parks.	Regional park, community/high-use urban park, neighborhood park, mini-park, greenway, and special facilties (historic sites, nature preserves, sports complexes)	Urban forest, urban parks, regional parks, neighborhood parks, habitat parks, community parks, community gardens, public gardens, and golf courses	Breathing Room Open Space, Usable Open Space, Greenspaces, and Offsets (not owned by department but used in the same manner as such city-owned facilities. Example: school grounds)	Defined as an "outdoor system" with these components: greenways, beaches, and scenic waterways; cultural and natural resources; parks and athletic fields; and trails. Parks are defined as neighborhood, community, or district parks, and school spaces and homeowner "semi-public" parks are also included.
Yes. City organization chart,department organization chart, park needs	No	Yes, financial resources, sub-area acreage and population distribution, and inventory and projected deficit areas.	Not included	Yes. Focus group results
Yes, GIS maps of planning areas and demographic profiles, historic maps, facilities and programs, universal access-related,	Yes. 11 maps of existing resources and proposed additions	Yes, park resources by subarea	Yes, in the Gap Analysis document	Yes. Planning areas
Yes. Inventory tables, facilities and programs tables, and needs tables	Yes. 31 tables of national, state, and local data. Also include public meeting comments and cost estimates.	Yes, comparative matrix of park sites to be developed and renovated by subarea.	Not included	Yes. Open space and recreation needs by planning area, land acquisition costs, future improvements, standards evaluation by planning area
Focused on public meeting comments and survey results. Also includes a bibliography.	3 appendices: Metro Parks and Greenways Design Guidelines for Metro Parks; Revenue enhancement for golf operations — Illustrative economics; and US Green Building Council LEED project checklist	Under separate cover, covering 7 topics including public participation process, history, inventory, level of service, program areas, park classifications, and specific technical reports (demographics, trends, etc.)	Companion document "An Assessment of Gaps in Seattle's Open Space Network" with 9 maps	No appendices
Yes. Documentation included in appendix.	Not noted in the plan.	Not noted in the plan.	Yes, officially adopted by City Council Resolution 30181	Yes, city council adopted a resolution to accept the plan as a guidance document for open space and recreational planning, and to integrate it as part of the city's next comprehensive plan.
None	www.nashville.gov/parks/master_plan.htm	http://www.portlandonline.com/parks/index.cfm?c=eabic	www.seattle.gov/parks/publications/plan2000.htm	None

TABLE B-2. PROGRAMMATIC ELEMENTS

PLAN JURISDICTION	ALEXANDRIA, VA	BELLEVUE, WA	DENVER, CO	EUGENE, OR
CONNECTION MADE TO OTHER PLANS/REPORTS/ LEGISLATION	Included as an element in 1978 comprehensive plan; 1992 plan update listed goals and objectives for parks but not a full element; these goals and objectives are referenced here.	1993 Parks and Open Space System Plan; Washington State Growth Management Act; City of Bellevue Comprehensive Plan; Recreation Program Plan; Pedestrian and Bicycle Transportation Plan Update; Downtown Needs Assessment and Downtown Implementation Plan; Human Services Needs Update; Historic and Cultural Resources Survey; Housing Needs Assessment for Disabled Report; Renovation and Refurbishment Plan; Sportsfield Analysis Report	Comprehensive Plan 2000, Blueprint Denver, Downtown Area Plan, Pedestrian Master Plan	Eugene-Springfield Metro Area General Plan
EXECUTIVE SUMMARY	Covers plan emphasis, need for the plan, goals, priority actions, sequence for implementation, and potential funding sources and strategies	Not included	Provides an overview of the contents of each chapter	Provides brief history, document outline, vision, mission, goals, list of strategies in all 9 strategy areas, funding options, and performance measures summary.
INTRODUCTION	Includes history of Alexandria and its open space, and the planning process used here	Chapter 1, Perspective, discusses creating and fulfilling the vision for parks	Not included	Includes planning process and needs assessment
VISION STATEMENT	A map of the physical vision for the system.	"City in a Park"; elaborated upon more in the Introduction	Not included explicitly; Chapter 1 sets out the vision for the entire plan.	"We envision an interconnected and accessible system of vibrant public spaces, friendly neighborhood parks, thriving natural areas and diverse recreation opportunities that make our city a healthy, active, and beautiful place in which to live, work, and play."

INDIANAPOLIS-MARION COUNTY, IN	NASHVILLE, TN	PORTLAND, OR	SEATTLE, WA	VIRGINIA BEACH, VA
Marion County Comprehensive Land-Use Plan; Regional Center Plan 2020; 2002 Greenways Plan; various neighborhood plans	Tennessee State Recreation Plan, Greenways for Nashville and Davidson County Action Plan	No mention of other plans	1993 COMPLAN (parks), 1994 Seattle Comprehensive Plan, Seattle Comprehensive Transportation Plan, Urban Wildlife Habitat Plan, Urban Trails Plan (pending as of 2000), and neighborhood plans (various)	Update to the 1994 plan and will be incorporated into the next comprehensive plan. Also addresses coordinating trails with the Princess Anne Corridor Plan
Not included	Covers the existing system, what is proposed, and the estimated cost	Lists the objectives of the plan, summarizes the 6 specific actions to be taken over the next 20 years, and lists recommendations on strategies to best implement the actions.	Not included	Includes summary of general description of system components, background information sources, citizen involvement techniques used, analysis process and results, organization of recommendations, implementation strategies, and recommended land acquisition and improvements for entire system
Background on agency, plan purpose, comprehensive planning, plan components, benefits of parks and recreation, planning process, and departmental organization and goals.	Includes benefits of parks and greenways, planning process overview, and list of technical studies completed to support the planning process	Includes the vision statement and nine guiding principles: essential element, connected system, inclusive and accessible, stewardship, intrinsic value, excellence, beauty and innovation, future needs, and civic involvement	Includes connection to other plans, especially the comprehensive plan and neighborhood plans, and purpose of this plan. It is an update to the 1993 parks plan	Not included
"Indy Parks shall provide safe, well-maintained parkland and natural areas. These lands shall provide quality recreation and environmental services that are models for all Marion County citizens. In support of strong neighborhoods, Indy Parks shall actively partner with recreation, environmental, and social service providers; educational institutions; and other government agencies in order to provide vital living links to our, and through our, parks to neigborhoods, schools and businesses. We will enhance a thriving economy by utilizing our natural, cultural, financial, and human resources in order to inspire a healthy lifestyle while celebrating cultural diversity and instilling a respect for the natural environment in which we live, work and play."	Excerpt: "The parks and recreation programs of Metropolitan Nashville and Davidson County will significantly enhance the quality of life in the community. Regardless of race, income or physical ability, citizens will have equal access to parks and recreation programs with a sense of personal safety. Citizens will enjoy an interconnected system of greenways, trails, natural areas, open spaces, and recreation facilities, distributed in response to need throughout the metropolitan region."	"Portland's parks, public places, natural areas and recreation opportunities give life and beauty to our city. These essential assets connect people to place, self and others. Portland's residents will treasure and care for this legacy, building on the past to provide for future generations."	"Seattle's parks and recreation system will be a neighborhood-based system of open space, parks, facilities, and programs that captures the spirit of Seattle's magnificent setting in the Olmsted tradition. Seattle's parks and recreation system will: be connected by boulevards, trails, public transportation, and green streets; encompass views and provide opportunities for the enjoyment of the vast water resources in Seattle; be linked closely with the City's neighborhoods, schools, and other city services; be maintained for public enjoyment, stewardship of resources and a healthy environment, and; be brought to life through programs, events, employees, and the efforts of volunteers."	"To develop an attractive, environmentally sensitive open space system to include trails, greenways and scenic waterways, beaches, parks, natural and agricultural areas, scenic road corridors, and attractive, pleasing places to live, work, and play." Plan also includes visions for each open space resource.

TABLE B-2. PROGRAMMATIC ELEMENTS (CONTINUED)

PLAN JURISDICTION	ALEXANDRIA, VA	BELLEVUE, WA	DENVER, CO	EUGENE, OR
DEPARTMENTAL MISSION STATEMENT	Not included	"A healthy community through an integrated system of exceptional parks, open space, recreation, cultural and human services."	Not included	"Strengthening our community by preserving and enhancing our parks and open space system and providing diverse recreation experiences."
PUBLIC PARTICIPATION	SC, PM, Open Space Summit	PM, PS, FG	PF, SC, FG, WEB, PS	PS, FG, PI, SC, IS
INVENTORY	Includes map of open space resources and a table. Detailed inventory in separate volume.	Expressed as total number of acres	Not detailed; described in number of acres/1,000 provided in each neighborhood, presented in map form.	Total number of acres of each park type presented in a table; also gives detail on number of acres of each park type for each subarea
LEVEL OF SERVICE (LOS)/ TYPE OF STANDARD	Acres per 1,000 population, and uses benchmark analysis of similar cities	NRPA Open Space standards with service area and park size. Discusses limitations of standards, and presents goal of park within 1/2 mile of every citizen	Unique LOS created based on four considerations: comparison cities, department expertise, NRPA standards, and resident surveys. Excludes golf courses from final evaluation. Includes providing parkland within 1/2 mile of every residence.	General standard of 20 acres/1,000 population. Based on national figures and local needs. Also addressed in distance per resident to a park (1/2 mile for neighborhood; 2 miles for community)

KEY TO ABBREVIATIONS IN TABLE B-2

PUBLIC PARTICIPATION METHODS	
Personal interviews	PI
Public surveys	PS
Public meetings	PM
Web based information	WEB
Steering Committee	SC
Focus Groups	FG
Information sessions	IS
Earlier plans	EP

INDIANAPOLIS-MARION COUNTY, IN	NASHVILLE, TN	PORTLAND, OR	SEATTLE, WA	VIRGINIA BEACH, VA
"Indy Parks shall provide clear leadership and well-defined direction for enhancing the quality of life for Indianapolis and Marion County residents by providing park and recreation resources and services that: provide and/or facilitate quality recreation and leisure opportunities; encourage and support natural and cultural resource stewardship and environmental education; include safe, clean, well-maintained park facilities for the community's use and enjoyment; promote and facilitate mutually beneficial county-wide partnerships."	"It is the mission of the Metropolitan Board of Parks and Recreation to provide every citizen of Nashville and Davidson County with an equal opportunity for safe recreational and cultural activities within a network of parks and greenways that preserves and protects the region's natural resources."	Mission statement not included, but seven principles are noted as part of the vision: essential element; connected system; inclusive and accessible; stewardship; intrinsic value; excellence; beauty and innovation; future needs; and civic involvement.	"Seattle Department of Parks and Recreation will work with all citizens to be good stewards of our environment, and to provide safe and welcoming opportunities to play, learn, contemplate and build community."	Not included
PS, PM, EP	PS, PM, SC	PM, PS, SC, and staff meetings	PM, IS, public hearing	FG, PS, PM
Table of inventory of parks, by park type.	Lists each park according to the park categories, and provides total park acreage for each park type by planning areas. Includes an extensive analysis section assessing the condition of existing resources.	Not included here, but plan states an inventory is in the appendices. Plan notes the total acreage generally and number of each type of open space.	Not included	Inventory is of current open space and city-owned and privately held vacant land. Counts are provided for each planning area.
Unique level of service for three park types (community parks, neighborhood parks, mini parks), developed in 2000 plan. Uses service area measurement (distance from residences).	NRPA and Metro Parks standard per 1,000 population. Also uses service area distances. Note that a service radius standard of 2 miles to a greenway is used.	Level of service defined citywide by acres per thousand population. Service areas for each park type (1/2 mile for each neighborhood park; 1 mile for each community park)	Called Distribution Guidelines, for each resource there is a desirable LOS, an acceptable LOS, and description of offsets. LOS is defined differently for the particular resource. For Breathing Room Open Space, the desirable LOS is 1 acre/100 population. Seattle Comprehensive Plan defines open space goals based on three development types: urban center villages, hub urban villages, and residential urban villages	For each planning area there is a standards evaluation chart, using state-level standards of 10 acres/1,000 population for all open space.

TABLE B-3. IMPLEMENTATION ELEMENTS

PLAN JURISDICTION	ALEXANDRIA, VA	BELLEVUE, WA	DENVER, CO	EUGENE, OR
GOALS	15 goals: • protect and enrich existing parks • develop innovative opportunities for creating additional open space • complete implementation of the Potomac River Waterfront Plan • protect and expand stream valleys and other sensitive areas • create an open space network in new development areas • protect and preserve institutional open space • create public open space from vacant land • link and expande bike, pedestrian, and trail systems • enhance streetscapes and gateways • maximize use of public school open space areas • expand citywide street tree program and protect existing trees and woodland areas • encourage the creation of civic parks at and adjacent to Metro stations • beautify interchanges and highway corridors • protect privately owned open space	Five objectives: • protect and preserve environmentally sensitive natural areas • provide connections for an integrated open space system • enhance the city's visual character throughout the park system • acquire and develop park facilities to meet present and future needs • renovate or modify parks for optimum use of resources.	10 goals: • increase parkland • increase tree canopy • water conservation • conserve other natural resources • improve access • consider recreation of the future and trends • more natural areas • preserve historic parks, parkways, and structures • revitalize mountain parks • change how department does business	13 goals: • outdoor opportunities • inclusive, accessible, and affordable programs and places • health and wellness; community partnerships • underserved populations • lifelong human development • environmental stewardship • understanding and sense of community • equitable distribution • sustainable parks, recreation, and open space • high quality natural areas • fiscal responsibility • efficient use of resources
ISSUES	Lack of open space continuity and connection, diminishing availability of open space, uneven distribution of open space, and need for stewardship and protection, especially in natural areas	Nine Focus Areas include open space, greenways, corridors, and trails; waterfront access; neighborhood sites; community parks; recreation facilities; downtown district; partnership opportunities; renovation, maintenance, and security; and historic, cultural and art resources	Street tree canopy, equitable park acreage, "green street" connections, regional trails, accessible urban waterways, natural areas, and increasing neighborhood "breathing space"	Balanced and equitable system, accessible and connection park system, renovation and maintenance of existing parks and facilities, youth asset development, and volunteering opportunities
NEEDS ASSESSMENT TOOLS (KEY TO ABBREVIATIONS APPEARS ON PAGE 104)	PP, DEM, PF. Separate study being conducted.	RS, FG, PF. This document is an update to the 1993 plan, and the focus areas are the same as the previous plan.	GGA, BA, SNG, DEM	DEM, GGA, PF, FG, RS, WS
SPECIAL NEEDS GROUPS	Not specifically mentioned	Yes, Seniors, youth, and disabled	Youth and elderly	Ethnic groups, specifically hispanic and Native American
ACTIONS	11 priority actions, derived from the open space summit. Section serves as actual implementation guidance.	Short- and long-term capital recommendations; recommendations by focus area	Based on the 4 values in the comprehensive plan: sustainability, equity, engagement, and sound economics	Defined by 9 strategy areas: recreation programs, parks, community facilities, natural areas access and connectivity, renovation/restoration, maintenance, resource development, and management

INDIANAPOLIS-MARION COUNTY, IN	NASHVILLE, TN	PORTLAND, OR	SEATTLE, WA	VIRGINIA BEACH, VA
6 priorities: • Sustainability and Environmental Education • Stewardship • Cultural Legacy • Mission Driven Services • Fitness and Health • Accessibility	5 goals: • Establish and maintain a regional system of public parks and greenways that provides recreation, educational, ecological, and aesthetic benefits to enhance the quality of life for all citizens • Offer all citizens opportunities to participate in cultural, athletic, and environmental programs • Design, operate and maintain safe parks and greenways • Meet financial needs of the regional parks system as measured by high levels of visitation, volunteer support services, and a willingness to commit the funds needed to establish and maintain facilities and programs • Encourage development of a network of open space throughout Davidson county that complements public parks and greenways	5 goals: • Ensure Portland's park and recreation legacy for future generations • provide a wide variety of high quality park and recreation services and opportunities for all residents • preserve, protect, and restore Portland's natural resources to provide "nature in the city" • create an interconnected regional and local system of trails, paths and walks to make Portland "the walking city of the West" • develop parks, recreation facilities and programs that promote community in the city (Multiple objectives listed for each goal, some quantifiable)	7 goals: • Habitat • Happiness • Harmony • Health • Heritage • Hospitality • Humanity	3 goals: • To make recommendations about open space in Virginia Beach, particularly in the northern area of the city threatened by infill development • to provide opportunities for citizen involvement and feedback in determining where open space should be acquired and what should be done with the land • to provide realistic funding recommendations based on citizen involvement and analysis
Providing adequate resources to increasing population on edge of jurisdiction	Parkland deficits in most planning areas, for both current and future populations, and overall condition of parks and facilities.	Changing population, increasing development, and demand for more recreation. Also mentions managing partnerships and better coordination with city and regional planning. Issues are defined more specifically for each subarea.	Policy statement section outlines specific items under two categories: Partner for Recreation, and Steward of Park Resources	Issues are to create or expand on natural areas and greenways; more active recreation parks, including more soccer fields and ballfields, more bike, equestrian, and pedestrian trails, and improve and increase access to public beaches (by providing more parking).
BA, NPT, PF, RS, GAP Includes maps of underserved areas and of potential concentrations of park users. Also includes budget and maintenance analysis, status of 2000 plan action items, and proposed land acquisition	PP, US, NPT, GGA, LPD, CC	PP, MOP, GGA	PP, LOSGA, DEM, GGA	LOSGA; 3 components to needs assessment: Statistical Inventory, Evaluation Criteria, and Fiscal Impact.
Universal Access chapter addresses needs of disabled	Not specifically mentioned	Not specifically mentioned	Youth, disabled, seniors, low-income households, non-English speakers, and ethnic populations	Not specifically mentioned
The 6 priorities organize the 65 identified action steps	Numerous actions listed, organized according to objectives under each goal.	7 strategy topics on governance, planning, partnership, development, marketing and communication, management, and funding. 6 immediate next steps: establish: a parks and recreation board and a parks foundation; develop: a 20-year capital plan; a marketing and community involvment plan; a partnership plan; and long- and short-term funding plans	6-year action plan for Partner for Recreation actions includes development of park and recreation facilities, management and maintenance of parks facilities, and recreation programs. Steward of Park Resources actions: acquisitions and development, park management and environmental stewardship, and education.	Recommendations are made for each planning area, for each of the resource types, and are aggregated into the 3 geographic areas

TABLE B-3. IMPLEMENTATION ELEMENTS (CONTINUED)

PLAN JURISDICTION	ALEXANDRIA, VA	BELLEVUE, WA	DENVER, CO	EUGENE, OR
IMPLEMENTATION	Recommendations and strategies for each of the 15 goals are included.	Not specified	Chapter 10, Next Steps: The Framework for Implementation covers the implementation strategy.	Included in the separate Project and Priority Plan, published in May 2006 (result of a 2-year public input process)
EVALUATION METHODS	Not specifically mentioned	Chapter 4 reviews projects completed and progress made since adopting the 1993 plan.	Describes an indicators and performance goals approach to addressing each of the 10 goal items, using the current status as the benchmark upon which to measure	Quantifiable performance measures included in chapter 6; updates on plan included on website.
FUNDING OPTIONS	Create an organization for fundraising and stewardship; establish funding for acquisition and development, including dedicated trusts and funds, bonds, taxes, and easements; establish funding for operations through corporate sponsorships and volunteer programs; and pursue public and institutional grants.	Includes traditional capital improvements plan (CIP) funding, voter initiatives, expanded user fees, King County Conservation futures tax, Real Estate Excise Tax, general obligation bonds, Councilmanic bonds, Revenue bonds, grants, partnerships, annexations, impact fees, parks and recreation service areas, and real estate transactions	Analyzes projected revenues, provides a breakdown of City of Denver general fund revenue and expenditures, capital need trends, and a table with expansion estimates (includes costs, potential partners, project size). Outlines potential funding resources and includes information on a survey completed on residents willingness to pay for park changes	Innovative measures considered include entertainment taxes, utility taxes, corporate income tax, income tax surcharge, personal income tax, gross receipts tax, payroll tax, general sales tax, restaurant tax, business license tax, new construction fees, and special county service district
BUDGET/ FORECASTING	No budget included, but plan does tie specific goals to each funding option	Includes projection of funding sources and revenues through 2009, CIP funding, and short-term revenue sources	Included generally, in a short narrative.	Included in Project and Priority Plan

KEY TO ABBREVIATIONS IN TABLE B-3

NEEDS ASSESSMENT TOOLS	
Population projections	PP
User/preference survey	US
Benchmark analysis of similar cities	BA
National participation trends data	NPT
Capacity calculations	CC
Public meetings or forums	PF
Workshops	WS
Focus groups	FG
Resident survey	RS
Special needs groups	SNG
Demographic trends and analysis	DEM
Geographic gap analysis	GGA
LOS gap analysis	LOSGA
Local participation data	LPD

INDIANAPOLIS-MARION COUNTY, IN	NASHVILLE, TN	PORTLAND, OR	SEATTLE, WA	VIRGINIA BEACH, VA
Combined with Actions. Focus is on capital improvements. No specific implementation program noted.	Not specified	20-year capital plan to be developed within 18 months of this plan's adoption. Plan to be implemented in a first 5-year, second 5-year, and third 10-year increment system.	In the document "An Assessment of Gaps in Seattle's Open Space Network," section called "How the City is Responding" covers implementation	Recommendations are ranked as top, high, or moderate priorities.
Annual review and update (when appropriate) of the five-year action plan, capital improvements plan, and acquisition plan. Annual soliciation of stakeholder input. Other methods indirectly related to plan implementation and update.	Plan update on departmental website	Not specifically mentioned	Not specifically mentioned	Virginia Beach Outdoors Plan Open Space Preservation Program Semi-Annual Report, published in January and July each year, provides information on open space acquisition and funding.
Capital improvements and estimated costs listed but funding sources are not included.	Not detailed. $35 million was appropriated for parks improvements.	Current sources include general fund, grants and donations, and the residential systems development charge. Potential sources include general obligation bonds, grants and gifts, local option tax, regional funding, niche taxes, and non-residential system development charge.	For capital projects, the cumulative reserve fund, neighborhood matching funds, and grant sources are noted as funding options. Indicates that additional funding must be sought, either levies or bond issues. Gap report indicates that a Pro Parks levy of $198.2 million was approved.	Funding options noted include bonds, pay as you go fees, adopting a tax increase of $60/year per household, and creating a designated fund for open space acquisition.
Not included	Operating budget impact of capital improvements plan, both revenues and expenses, included.	Basic outline of costs and current shortfall in funding included	Not included	Included, with a rough estimate of costs